Lecture Notes
in Business Information Processing　　　**439**

Series Editors

Wil van der Aalst ⓘ
  RWTH Aachen University, Aachen, Germany

John Mylopoulos ⓘ
  University of Trento, Trento, Italy

Sudha Ram ⓘ
  University of Arizona, Tucson, AZ, USA

Michael Rosemann ⓘ
  Queensland University of Technology, Brisbane, QLD, Australia

Clemens Szyperski
  Microsoft Research, Redmond, WA, USA

More information about this series at https://link.springer.com/bookseries/7911

Daniel Mendez · Manuel Wimmer ·
Dietmar Winkler · Stefan Biffl ·
Johannes Bergsmann (Eds.)

Software Quality

The Next Big Thing in Software Engineering and Quality

14th International Conference on Software Quality, SWQD 2022
Vienna, Austria, May 17–19, 2022
Proceedings

Editors
Daniel Mendez ⓘ
Blekinge Institute of Technology
Karlskrona, Sweden

Manuel Wimmer ⓘ
Johannes Kepler University of Linz
Linz, Austria

Dietmar Winkler ⓘ
TU Wien
Vienna, Austria

Stefan Biffl ⓘ
TU Wien
Vienna, Austria

Johannes Bergsmann
Software Quality Lab GmbH
Linz, Austria

ISSN 1865-1348   ISSN 1865-1356 (electronic)
Lecture Notes in Business Information Processing
ISBN 978-3-031-04114-3   ISBN 978-3-031-04115-0 (eBook)
https://doi.org/10.1007/978-3-031-04115-0

This Springer imprint is published by the registered company Springer Nature Switzerland AG
The registered company address is: Gewerbestrasse 11, 6330 Cham, Switzerland

Message from the General Chair

The Software Quality Days (SWQD) conference and tools fair was first organized in 2009 and has since grown to be the largest yearly conference on software quality in Europe with a strong and vibrant community. The program of the SWQD conference was designed to encompass a stimulating mixture of practice-oriented presentations, scientific presentations of new research topics, tutorials, and an exhibition area for tool vendors and other organizations in the area of software quality.

This professional symposium and conference aims to offer a range of comprehensive and valuable opportunities for advanced professional training, new ideas, and networking with a series of keynote speeches, professional lectures, exhibits, and tutorials.

The SWQD conference welcomes anyone interested in quality in the whole software life cycle including the following: software process and quality managers, test managers, software testers, product managers, agile masters, project managers, software architects, software designers, requirements engineers, user interface designers, software developers, IT managers, release managers, development managers, application managers, and many more.

The guiding conference topic of SWQD 2022 was "What's The Next Big Thing in Software Engineering and Quality?", as changed product, process, and service requirements, e.g., distributed engineering projects, mobile applications, involvement of heterogeneous disciplines and stakeholders, extended application areas, and new technologies, include new challenges and might require new and adapted methods and tools to support quality activities in the software life cycle.

May 2022   Johannes Bergsmann

Message from the Scientific Program Chairs

The 14th Software Quality Days (SWQD) conference and tools fair brought together researchers and practitioners from business, industry, and academia working on quality assurance and quality management for software engineering and information technology. The SWQD conference is one of the largest software quality conferences in Europe.

Over the past years, we have received a growing number of scientific contributions to the SWQD conference. Since 2012, the SWQD conference has included a dedicated scientific program published in scientific proceedings. In this 14th edition, we received a total of eight high-quality submissions from researchers across Europe which were each peer reviewed by four or more reviewers. Out of these submissions, we selected four contributions as full papers. These accepted papers were then added to the already established program from the previous edition, which had to be postponed in light of the COVID-19 pandemic, yielding a rich program full of presentations and interactive sessions.

The main topics from academia and industry in the new accepted manuscripts are about the application of artificial intelligence for software engineering problems as well as quality assurance for software-intensive systems.

May 2022

Daniel Mendez
Manuel Wimmer

Organization

Organizing Committee

SWQD 2022 was organized by Software Quality Lab GmbH, the Institute of Information Systems Engineering at TU Wien, the Blekinge Institute of Technology, and the Johannes Kepler University Linz.

General Chair

Johannes Bergsmann   Software Quality Lab GmbH, Austria

Scientific Program Chairs

Daniel Mendez   Blekinge Institute of Technology, Sweden, and fortiss GmbH, Germany

Manuel Wimmer   Johannes Kepler University Linz, Austria

Steering Committee

Stefan Biffl   TU Wien, Austria

Dietmar Winkler   TU Wien, Austria

Daniel Mendez   Blekinge Institute of Technology, Sweden, and fortiss GmbH, Germany

Manuel Wimmer   Johannes Kepler University Linz, Austria

Johannes Bergsmann   Software Quality Lab GmbH, Austria

Organizing and Publicity Chair

Petra Bergsmann   Software Quality Lab GmbH, Austria

Program Committee

SWQD 2022 established an international committee of well-known experts in software quality to peer review the scientific submissions.

Matthias Book   University of Iceland, Iceland

Ruth Breu   University of Innsbruck, Austria

Tomas Bures   Charles University, Czech Republic

Maya Daneva   University of Twente, The Netherlands

Contents

Contents

Invited Papers

Continuous Software Engineering in the Wild

Eriks Klotins[1]([✉]) [iD] and Tony Gorschek[1,2] [iD]

[1] Software Engineering Research Lab (SERL), Blekinge Institute of Technology,
Karlskrona, Sweden
{eriks.klotins,tony.gorschek}@bth.se
[2] fortiss GmbH, Munich, Germany

Abstract. Software is becoming a critical component of most products and organizational functions. The ability to continuously improve software determines how well the organization can respond to market opportunities. Continuous software engineering promises numerous advantages over sprint-based or plan-driven development. However, implementing a continuous software engineering pipeline in an existing organization is challenging.

In this invited position paper, we discuss the adoption challenges and argue for a more systematic methodology to drive the adoption of continuous engineering. Our discussion is based on ongoing work with several industrial partners as well as experience reported in both state-of-practice and state-of-the-art.

We conclude that the adoption of continuous software engineering primarily requires analysis of the organization, its goals, and constraints. One size does not fit all purposes, meaning that many of the principles behind continuous engineering are relevant for most organizations, but the level of realization and the benefits may still vary. The main hindrances to continuous flow of software arise from sub-optimal organizational structures and the lack of alignment. Once those are removed, the organization can implement automation to further improve the software delivery.

Keywords: Continuous software engineering · Process improvement · Continuous integration and delivery

1 Introduction

Software is a critical component of most products, services, manufacturing processes, and back-office functions. The ability to continuously improve software is crucial for organizations to respond to market opportunities swiftly and remain competitive. Software is also becoming increasingly more complex. Organizations seek to improve both the effectiveness and the efficiency of software engineering to enable further growth without increasing overhead and losing flexibility.

Continuous software engineering is a paradigm aiming to streamline software engineering by delivering software frequently and in small increments, and by

© Springer Nature Switzerland AG 2022
D. Mendez et al. (Eds.): SWQD 2022, LNBIP 439, pp. 3–12, 2022.
https://doi.org/10.1007/978-3-031-04115-0_1

doing so reaping different benefits from fast customer feedback, to continuous value delivery to said customers. Smaller increments are potentially easier to plan, develop, integrate, and verify. On the customers' side, more minor updates ought to create less disruption and are easier to adopt in contrast to big-bang software updates requiring downtime and catching up with the new features. Software vendors can collect more focused telemetry and customer feedback to steer further product development [2]. More frequent and smaller software updates enable customers to provide more focused feedback empowering them to participate in steering the product more actively. In turn, this allows collaborative and experience-based business models [2].

Continuous integration and delivery (CI/CD) is part of continuous software engineering. We consider how organizations can apply continuous principles throughout the whole software engineering process throughout inception, development, integration, verification, delivery, operation, use, collection of feedback, and planning the next software iteration steps [1].

However, few organizations have adopted continuous engineering beyond automating tests and other repetitive development tasks. To the best of our knowledge, an industrial-scale end-to-end pipeline from inception of a feature to collecting and analyzing customer feedback has yet to be demonstrated in peer-reviewed literature [7].

The potential benefits of continuous software engineering have gained much attention. Benefits like flexibility, efficiency, and improved time-to-market are appealing to most companies. However, the ability to retrofit an existing organization, what parameters determine the suitability, and what trade-offs are associated with adopting continuous software engineering remain largely unexplored.

This invited position paper discusses the potential, and highlights challenges hindering the widespread adoption of continuous software engineering. This is a position paper based on ongoing research with a dozen companies from multiple domains, featuring different market positions and customers, as part of the KKS research profile project Software Engineering Rethought (see http://rethought.se).

Overall, we observe that end-to-end continuous software engineering, as per many recommendations, may not be applicable everywhere [1, 2]. However, organizations can adopt parts of the pipeline to streamline software engineering [4]. The challenge lies in the critical evaluation of the current situation and the goals of the company to maximize the gains from adopting continuous software engineering principles.

This paper is structured as follows: Sect. 2 presents the potential of an end-to-end continuous software engineering. In Sect. 3, we discuss challenges and the need for further research, before concluding our paper in Sect. 4.

2   Continuous Software Engineering in a Nutshell

The idea of continuous software engineering originates from lean principles in manufacturing. One of the key principles in lean is to reduce waste and maximize customer value by implementing the flow. That is, linking all relevant production steps together and minimizing the lead time of each step. In software engineering, this principle can be implemented by delivering small increments of software [6].

To enable the development and delivery of small software increments, software vendors need to implement a software delivery pipeline. The pipeline picks up the latest changes in the source code and automatically performs testing, integration, delivery, and other required steps to make the latest changes available to end-users. Once end-users start using the software, feedback and telemetry is relayed back to the software vendor for analysis and decision support to steer further product decisions.

In an idealized scenario, end-users gain access to the latest features and start generating feedback minutes after developers have finished the development [1,2].

The state-of-the-art view on the end-to-end pipeline, along with the key steps, is shown in Fig. 1. The figure shows an idealized scenario that requires adaptations to fit any real-life scenario.

In the figure, we show the key steps of the pipeline denoted with rectangular boxes. The arrows represent the flow of software and related artifacts through the pipeline. Dashed lines represent levels of stakeholders involved in product development.

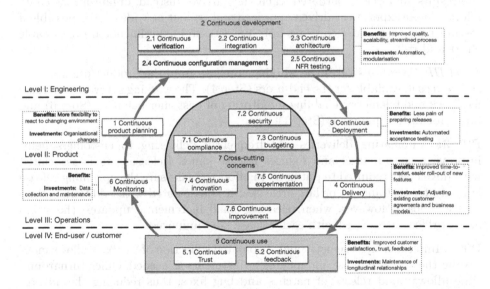

Fig. 1. An overview of state-of-the-art continuous software engineering pipeline

We differentiate between four levels of stakeholders, present how continuous software engineering affects each level, and present several potential opportunities (**PT**) associated with adopting continuous engineering. The PT's are idealized positive outcomes that can be a result of realizing good continuous practices, used here to highlight potential benefits only for illustration purposes.

Level I: Engineering organization receives plans from the product planning organization and turns these plans into working software for deployment (Step 3). The engineering organization implements build, test, integration, and deployment automation; ensures the organization and software architecture supports incremental and parallel work. Note that the exact engineering activities are case-specific. In the figure, we illustrate the most common activities.

PT 1: Automation and parallel work on small increments are shown to improve efficiency quality, reduce stress and improve developer satisfaction. Independent, cross-functional teams taking responsibility for specific features and modular architectures allow scaling of development organization with minimal need for additional overhead.

Level II: Product organization uses various inputs to devise plans for further product development (Step 2). These plans guide the engineering organization. Once the engineering is complete, the engineering organization returns working software (Step 3).

PT 2: Working with lightweight plans and quick turnaround time allows product organization to rapidly adjust and explore new market opportunities. In dynamic markets, extensive market research and analysis could be counterproductive as the results are already outdated when they arrive. Instead, organizations could adopt a more experiment-driven approach and try out new ideas. It is possible if testing new ideas and recovering from unsuccessful experiments are reasonable effort and risk.

Level III: Operations takes the working software from the product organization and makes it available for the end-users (Step 4). The working software generates feedback and telemetry, enabling monitoring of customer behavior (Step 6) and input for further planning (Step 1).

PT 3: Automating deliveries and frequently delivering to customers helps improve time-to-market and reduces release pains. Release pain is associated with developers required to put in extra effort to make sure the upcoming release is ready for customers. For large releases, it is associated with additional stress and workload. However, when releasing small incremental updates, the stress and workload associated with each release are minimized.

PT 4: Implementing telemetry and automated collection of feedback allows monitoring the software in use and making adjustments as needed. Quick turnaround time allows rapid release of patches and bug fixes, thus reducing the adverse effects of slipped defects. From the customers perspective, automated, seamless updates remove the need to update the software manually.

Level IV: End-user/customer organization receives and uses the software (Step 5). Frequent upgrades and continuous access to new features enable service and experience-oriented business models. Such models encourage trust (Step 5.1), and the end-users are incentivised to actively participate in the product development by providing feedback (Step 5.2).

PT 5: Both customers and the vendor can benefit from more closer experience and service based collaboration model. It facilitated trust and created incentives for customers not to switch to another vendor.

Cross-cutting concerns transcends organizational levels. For instance, continuous improvement (Concern 7.6) attempts to measure and fine-tune the whole cycle continuously. Continuous experimentation allows a product organization to set up quick experiments to test market responses to new ideas (Concern 7.5).

PT 6: Continuous collection of data and frequent execution of the delivery process allows to systematically and continuously improve the process with every iteration.

PT 7: Transparency in planning and road maps of the development company can achieve a number of benefits. (i) Internal coordination in the development organization of what is in the pipe short- and medium term. (ii) Customers can be prepared of what is coming to prepare and plan for changes and benefits. (iii) Customers and the development organization can rather via transparency act as partners as interested customers can be active in the planning and release work.

In summary, adopting an end-to-end continuous software delivery pipeline as shown in Fig. 1 allows the software vendor to increase internal efficiency and streamline value creation.

3   Challenges and Future Needs

Despite many potential advantages, the utilization of continuous software engineering remains scarce relative to plan-driven or sprint-based engineering models. Several of our partner companies have started adopting initiatives moving towards continuous software engineering. However, the adoption is far from straightforward and hindered by many challenges. In this section, we present challenges that, in our view and experience, should be solved to support an industry-wide adoption of continuous engineering principles.

Challenge 0: Should you do it? The tendency to go for one-size-fits-all solutions and the power of "the next thing everyone is doing" can cause as much damage as benefit. A key is to start with an analysis of both the capacity and goals of the development organization, as well as the capacity and needs of the customer's organizations.

The development organization needs to specify goals and to break down these goals to a level where success (or failure) to achieve these goals can be "measured" by the organization, continuously as changes are realized. This is paramount to a risk analysis, and also a cost benefit analysis anchored in reality and objective observations. A significant bonus is that this activity also enables creating a common understanding of the potential, implications and direction of the changes from items impacting individual teams, to entire departments and the whole organization, as well as how they are dependent and tie together. In this, it is important to separate between the treatment (change/tool/action/new way of working) and the goals and attainment of the goals to enable an evidence-based change continuously.

At the same time, knowing your customer and the impact of continuous on them and the relationship with them is critical. What is the benefit for the customer? Is the domain and agreements between the customer and the development company suitable for a continuous environment? One specific example could be if the customer wants continuous changes in the product, and is there a tele-metrics/data feedback system in place to report on new features and changes enabling feedback? In some domains and for some development organizations a continuous model is non-controversial, but in some other domains most of the benefits attained via try-and-learn-improve are impossible to achieve. For example, an organization and customer operating in (even partly) safety-critical products, or where down-time of products incur substantial consequences, the benefit/risk/cost calculation is significantly different.

Significant research needs to be conducted, and usable and useful models need to be developed, to establishing cost-effective ways to continuously evaluate and course correct the continuous changes needed to achieve a continuous product development environment; maybe inspired by a hierarchically connected Goal-Question-Metric model [3] - back-filled by metrics and data collected via the continuous feedback cycle. As such, a goal and measurement program is created (and scaled to be usable and useful for the organization in question) and it is important to realize that it might lead to the conclusion that continuous engineering in its entirety and complete idealized form might not fit your organization. However, there are probably many parts of continuous engineering that are beneficial for most organizations. Start there.

Challenge 1: Determining Adoption Goals and Constraints. We observe that organizations often put forward aims like improving speed and efficiency to drive the adoption of continuous engineering. However, such aims are too vague to be measured and drive systematic improvements. When interpreted by different parts of the organization, vague goals may come at odds, or even worse result in different interpretations of said goals resulting in different direction of work and sub-optimizations.

For example, an R&D unit could interpret the efficiency as maximizing the delivery of new experimental features. For operations, efficiency could mean minimizing resources to ensure services availability. Without a joint view of what efficiency means and how it is measured in the given organizational context, internal deadlocks may arise, hindering the company's adoption effort and optimal operation.

Attaining specific goals often imply trade-offs. As in the earlier example, it could be challenging to launch many innovative features and reach high stability of services simultaneously. Such trade-offs need to be identified and analyzed to understand the associated constraints and degrees of freedom.

The analysis of organizational goals, constraints, and trade-offs should drive the organizational change towards continuous software engineering. One powerful tool in coordinating an organization, and making goals clear is to break-down goals into measurable effects or metrics. This requires a number of steps. The terms "value", "efficiency", or "effectiveness" need to be defined for each part of the organization [3]. These definitions need to be coordinated and streamlined - in essence shared. Then, metrics on how to ascertain level of success have to be detailed very early. How to measure if you are improving towards a goal is a prerequisite before adopting any treatment or change. For example, if you say a specific practice or set of practices should be realized to improve customer value, what type of customer value, and how do you measure it? This analysis would also pinpoint bottlenecks, inefficiencies, and areas of improvement, in addition to acting as a coordinating force as an organization realizes changes. You need to be able to measure benefits of a change as well as you measure the cost of said change.

Challenge 2: Considering the Return-of-Investment Perspective. Retrofitting an organization with a new continuous engineering pipeline and new ways of working is a substantial investment. The investments should be justified with potential benefits and be aligned with organizational objectives (Challenge 1). Notably, the organization must be prepared to realize the potential and materialize the benefits.

For example, an organization may invest in data collection (PT 5) and gain the potential of improved data-driven decisions (PT 2). However, if the rest of the organization is not ready to use the data in decision support, the potential is not realized, and the investment is wasted. Furthermore, customers may be slow in adopting new features, thus delaying the feedback and nullifying its value to the organization.

The organization should perform a cost-benefit analysis to gauge the viability of any goals, new practices, and working methods. Adoption champions should do such analysis in parallel with determining adoption goals, trade-offs, and constraints, see Challenge 1.

To address Challenges 1–2, we propose a model supporting inventory of goals, trade-offs, and return-of-investment calculation to support the systematic adoption of continuous practices. As a part of this analysis, the break-down of goals into defining the terms used to establish a common vocabulary, then establishing how to "measure" goal attainment by breaking down goals into measurable items. This also allows for course corrections during the changes associated with retrofitting.

Challenge 3: Focus on Cost Savings Instead of Value and Potential Creation. Our industry partners often mention the need to reduce cost and improve efficiency (PT 1) as reasons for considering continuous software engineering. Potential benefits like new value streams, improved time-to-market, and new business models are rarely, if at all, mentioned.

The question if adopting continuous practices would provide some cost savings is flawed. We compare such a question to asking whether eating healthier will be cheaper. Both eating healthier and adopting continuous engineering will likely cost more. Developing tests, maintaining test suites and automation infrastructure, collecting and maintaining test data, refactoring software architectures, and driving organizational adjustments will push the overall cost of software engineering upwards. At the same time, speed and flexibility will open up opportunities for new offerings enabling the organization to become faster at responding to market opportunities, among other benefits. Eating healthier may cost more, but may enable you a better and longer life.

We propose emphasizing the business value arising from streamlining software delivery over the exclusive focus on potential cost savings. More cross-disciplinary studies are needed to explore the business value perspective. We observe that continuous shares many characteristics with so called "digital transformation". Considering how continuous engineering fits into the broader organizational transformation could help to shift the focus from cost savings to unlocking the organizational potential [5].

Challenge 4: Remembering Conway's Law. In 1967, M. Conway formulated an adage that organizations develop systems that mimic their communication structure. In software engineering terms, software architecture should follow organizational structures. To change the prior, one needs to change the latter first.

Best practices of continuous software engineering dictate that development work should be done by real cross-functional teams that own the development of whole features. A team should have full responsibility from generating improvement ideas to development, testing, delivery, and telemetry analysis. This practice allows maintaining a modular architecture and to minimize the gap between organizational structures and software architectures.

From discussions with our partner companies, we learned that organizations often find their software architectures monolithic and poorly suited for parallel development, automation, and modular deployments. The software travels through various organizational silos, each performing a specific function without the complete picture. Handover from one silo to another creates friction and bottlenecks.

Attempts to break the software monolith often lead to failure as the surrounding organization remains the same. Changing the organizational structures is often extremely challenging due to internal inertia and resistance to changes.

We propose to explore the adoption of continuous engineering practices from the organizational view first. That is, analyze what organization silos and bottlenecks currently limit the continuous flow of software. Once organizational inefficiencies are addressed, the software delivery process can be further improved with tools such as automation. In addition, the detailed goals and following follow-up (metrics) should be owned by the parts of the organization (the teams) that own the module or part of the architecture. This way you can measure the fit of the organization to the goals of development. For example, a change in organizational structure might result in (metric) less waiting times between teams.

Challenge 5: Ever-Increasing Complexity. Contemporary market-driven software engineering exists in a dynamic environment. It faces mercurial market influences, changing organizational goals, technologies, and the growing size and complexity of software and the surrounding organization.

A single person, or a small group of people, can no longer grasp the complexity and make optimal and timely decisions using their expertise alone. This increase in complexity has far-reaching implications for how organizations make decisions.

One viable way forward could be to consider data collection and analysis as an integral part of the product and the engineering process. The organization can use data to support decisions both on what features to develop (*What to build?*) and how to improve the engineering process (*How to build?*).

Furthermore, retrospective analysis, that is, analyzing past events, has limited use in an increasingly changing environment. There is a potential to explore the applicability of inferential statistical methods, simulations, and machine learning techniques to make relevant predictions. This is however subject to significant research initiative to develop transparent tools and methods that can be trusted by practitioners to predict and simulate developments, at least in the short-term.

4 Conclusions

This invited position paper analyzes continuous software engineering and pinpoints several challenges of adopting ongoing software engineering from our collaboration with industrial partners. The challenges emphasize the need for systematic methods to analyze organizational goals, context, structures, constraints, among other contextual factors, to remove inefficiencies and realize the full potential of software-intensive products and services.

We wish to highlight that most inefficiencies and obstacles to streamlined value delivery can be traced to the lack of organizational alignment and coordination. The spirit of continuous engineering is to identify and remove such hindrances systematically. In the end, continuous software engineering is more about being pragmatic and disciplined in engineering than it is about automation.

References

1. Fitzgerald, B., Stol, K.J.: Continuous software engineering: a roadmap and agenda. J. Syst. Softw. **123**, 176–189 (2017)
2. Humble, J., Kim, G.: Accelerate: The science of lean software and DevOps: Building and scaling high performing technology organizations. IT Revolution (2018)
3. Khurum, M., Gorschek, T., Wilson, M.: The software value map-an exhaustive collection of value aspects for the development of software intensive products. J. Softw. Evol. Process **25**(7), 711–741 (2013)
4. Klotins, E., Gorschek, T.: Towards cost-benefit evaluation for continuous* software engineering activities. Rev. Empir. Softw. Eng. J. (2021)
5. Klotins, Eriks, P.A.E.: The unified perspective of digital transformation and continuous software engineering. In: Proceedings of 5th International Workshop on Software-Intensive Business (IWSIB) (2022)

6. Poppendieck, M., et al.: Principles of lean thinking. IT Manage. Select **18**(2011), 1–7 (2011)
7. Shahin, M., Babar, M.A., Zhu, L.: Continuous integration, delivery and deployment: a systematic review on approaches, tools, challenges and practices. IEEE Access **5**, 3909–3943 (2017)

Motivations for and Benefits of Adopting the Test Maturity Model integration (TMMi)

Erik van Veenendaal[1], Vahid Garousi[2,3], and Michael Felderer[4(✉)]

[1] TMMi Foundation, Chester, UK
erik@erikvanveenendaal.nl
[2] Queen's University Belfast, Belfast, UK
v.garousi@qub.ac.uk
[3] Bahar Software Engineering Consulting Limited, Carrickfergus, UK
[4] University of Innsbruck, Innsbruck, Austria
michael.felderer@uibk.ac.at

Abstract. Test Maturity Model integration (TMMi) is a popular model for maturity assessment and capability improvement of software testing practices in industry. Originally inspired by the Capability Maturity Model Integration (CMMI), and managed by the TMMi Foundation, the TMMi specification provides guidelines for assessing and improving testing capabilities of teams and organizations. In this invited paper, we discuss motivations for and benefits of adopting the TMMi. The discussion is based on an international user survey, which received data from 74 companies that have received TMMi assessments and certifications.

Keywords: Test Maturity Model integration · TMMi · Test process improvement · Software quality · Software testing

1 Introduction

In response to the growing demand for software quality and productivity, various initiatives, models, and approaches have been presented in the software industry since the 1980's. Examples include the Capability Maturity Model Integration (CMMI) model (cmmiinstitute.com) and the ISO/IEC 15504 standard, also known as the Software Process Improvement and Capability Determination (SPICE) model.

Over the past three decades, CMMI adoption has gradually increased, mostly for organizations working in governmental and defense projects. According to the CMMI Institute (cmmiinstitute.com/learning/appraisals/results), more than 10,000 companies have received CMMI appraisals (certifications).

While studies have reported that models such as CMMI and SPICE are useful, their primary focus is process improvements on the "overall" software development process lifecycle (SDLC). Despite the fact that software testing often accounts for a non-trivial portion of a typical software project in terms of time, budget and costs, such process improvement models do not provide specific improvement recommendations

© Springer Nature Switzerland AG 2022
D. Mendez et al. (Eds.): SWQD 2022, LNBIP 439, pp. 13–19, 2022.
https://doi.org/10.1007/978-3-031-04115-0_2

for software testing. For this reason, various models have been developed for dedicated improvements of software testing practices. A 2018 survey paper in IEEE Software [1] reported a catalog of 58 models for test maturity and capability improvements, e.g., the Test Maturity Model integration (TMMi) (tmmi.org), which, according to the paper [1], was the most widely used model.

Originally inspired by the CMMI, and managed by the TMMi Foundation, the TMMi model provides guidelines for assessing and improving testing capabilities. According to the internal assessments database of the TMMi Foundation, in total, 261 companies/teams were assessed in 28 countries by the end of 2021.

Since its inception in 2010, the TMMi Foundation has been proactive in promoting the usage of the TMMi and also in surveying its members and certified companies to track the state of the test maturity worldwide. One recent such activity was an international user survey of companies who have received the TMMi certifications. 74 companies participated in the survey by providing data. We report and discuss some of the results from that survey, focusing on motivations for and benefits of adopting the TMMi.

This invited paper is organized as follows. Section 2 provides a brief overview of TMMi. Section 3 discusses motivations for adopting TMMi. Section 4 discusses benefits of adopting TMMi. Finally, Sect. 5 concludes the paper.

2 A Brief Overview of TMMi

The roots of TMMi reach back to Gelperin and Hetzel's evolutionary testing model [2], published in 1988, and an early test improvement model named Test Maturity Model (TMM) [3]. By seeing the need for a more established test improvement model, several test and quality experts (volunteers) came together (mainly based in Europe) and founded the TMMi Foundation in 2010. The first stable version of the TMMi specification (version 1.0) was published by the Foundation in 2012 [4]. The latest version of the specification, as of this writing, is 1.2 [5], published in 2018. The TMMi Foundation is supported by the so-called TMMi Local Chapters that publicize and organize TMMi-related services and activities locally in their country or region. At the time of this writing, 26 TMMi Local Chapters, together covering 54 countries, are in existence, e.g., in China, the USA, Spain, Brazil, and France.

TMMi uses the concept of maturity levels for process evaluation and improvement. Furthermore, for each maturity level, a set of process areas, goals, and practices are identified. TMMi is aligned with international testing standards, syllabi, and terminology of the International Software Testing Qualifications Board (ISTQB), which has certified over 770,000 test professionals (October 2021). With TMMi, organizations can have their test processes objectively evaluated by accredited assessors and improve their test processes.

TMMi has a "staged" scheme for test process assessment and improvement. It contains stages or levels through which an organization passes as its testing process evolves from one that is ad-hoc, also called "initial or unmanaged" (level = 1) to one that is managed (level = 2), defined (level = 3), measured (level = 4), and optimized (level =

5). TMMi has five maturity levels. Each of them has several Process Areas (PA). Achieving each level ensures that the requirements (all process areas) of that level have been achieved. Each PA has several specific goals (SG) and specific practices (SP). Across the five levels, there are in total 16 PAs, 50 specific goals (SG), and 173 specific practices (SP). Details of those elements can be found in the TMMi framework [5].

For instance, under maturity level 2 ("managed"), there are five process areas, e.g., PA 2.1 (Test policy and strategy). This PA has three SGs: SG 1 (Establish a test policy), SG 2 (Establish a test strategy), and SG 3 (Establish test performance indicators). The above SG 1, in turn, has three SPs: SP 1.1 (Define test goals), SP 1.2 (Define test policy), and SP 1.3 (Distribute the test policy to stakeholders).

A main underlying principle of the TMMi is that it is a "generic" model applicable to various lifecycle models and environments. Several experience reports and case studies from the industrial application of TMMi have been published, e.g., [6] and [7].

In a recent IEEE Software paper [8], we presented a status report about TMMi, the trends of worldwide test maturity and certifications, and how companies have been ranked in each of its process areas (PA's). Our analysis showed that, since starting the TMMi assessments in 2011, the number of annual assessments has been between 15–30 companies each year. In 2019 (20 formal assessments), 2020 (28 formal assessments) and 2021 (39 formal assessments), there has already been a considerable growth in the uptake of the TMMi. We also found that for TMMi levels 2 and 3, PA2.5 (Test environment) and PA3.4 (Non-functional testing) have relatively more "not achieved" scores compared to other PAs. It seems that most companies have challenges in satisfying these two PAs. The important aspects of what the motivations for and benefits of adopting the TMMi are had not been systematically investigated so far, and that is the goal of our recent 2020 user survey, from which the current paper has been written.

3 Reasons (Motivations) for Adopting TMMi

Figure 1 shows the respondents' opinions on reasons for adopting TMMi. Enhancing software quality, increasing testing productivity, and reducing product risk were mentioned as the top three reasons, which essentially form the project management's "golden triangle". This indicates better management of testing is an important motivation to adopt TMMi. Furthermore, achieving TMMi certification is a key motivation for adopting TMMi, which indicates the importance of certification among TMMi certified organizations and their business operations. Good engineering practices like standardized compliance, delivery predictability and improved test engineering discipline are of moderate importance for motivating the adoption of TMMi. Meeting customer requirements, improving team morale, accelerating software delivery, and improving business alignment provide only a low motivation for adoption. Finally, reducing project costs provides the lowest motivation to adopt TMMi.

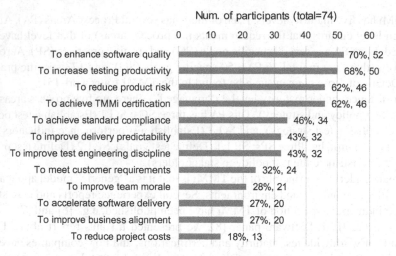

Fig. 1. Motivations for adopting TMMi.

4 Benefits of Adopting TMMi

Figures 2 and 3 show the results on benefits of adopting TMMi. Enhancing software quality, increasing testing productivity, and reducing product risk are not only high motivations but actually also observed benefits of adopting TMMi, by the responding organizations. Achieving TMMi certification is also reported to be a benefit. An interesting finding is that the internal factors of improved test engineering discipline and improved team morale are reported to be major benefits but were only moderate motivations to introduce TMMi. They can almost be considered "free" bonus when implementing TMMi.

Reduced project costs are not only the least motivation but also the least experienced benefit of adopting TMMi. This might indicate that TMMi is not suitable for organizations where reducing project cost is significantly more important than enhancing product quality, engineering discipline, or compliance. It may also indicate that since there is little motivation, the opportunities that are offered within TMMi to reduce projects costs are not in focus and/or not given priority.

The list of motivations/benefits from the survey was designed such that they can be categorized under six headings: product quality, test efficiency, compliance, people, test predictability, and business alignment. For example, reduced product risks and reduced number of defects both contribute to product quality, increased testing productivity contributes to test efficiency, and an improved test engineering discipline and improved team morale contribute to the people aspect. Changing the view from the individual benefits to the categorized one provided the outcome shown in Fig. 4.

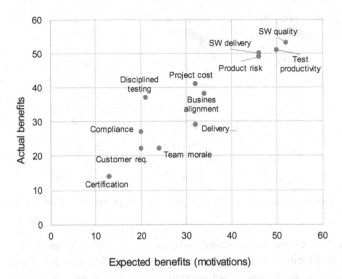

Fig. 2. Expected versus actual benefits when adopting TMMi.

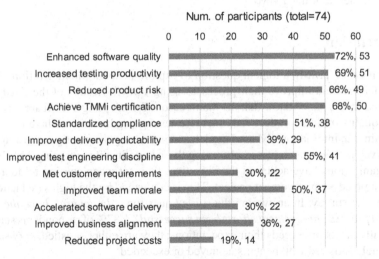

Fig. 3. Benefits of adopting TMMi.

A high 88% of the TMMi users are observing benefits for product quality (e.g., reduced product risks and/or reduced number of defects). Benefits are also commonly observed in terms of test efficiency (77%), compliance (84%), and regarding the people aspect (77%). Test predictability and business alignment both have a lower score. One should understand that test predictability is not fully achieved with practices such as test estimation and test project tracking at TMMi levels 2 and 3. Practices at higher TMMi levels, e.g., measurement (in level 4) and quality control (in level 5), are often needed to achieve test predictability. Hence, only when companies achieve TMMi level 4 or 5,

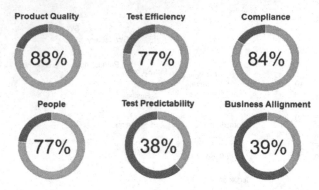

Fig. 4. Ration of respondents which reported different benefits of adopting TMMi.

test predictability benefits are observed and experienced. Also, when business alignment is low in the motivation list, the opportunities that are offered within TMMi to provide business alignment are probably not enough in focus. It is also an indicator that more specific practices on achieving business alignment (and value) should perhaps be present in the next release of the TMMi.

5   Conclusion

In the context of TMMi, a logical question to explore is about the motivations of companies to assess and improve their processes using TMMi. Results of the 2020 survey, as reported in this paper, show that the main reasons for adopting TMMi are to: enhance product quality, reduce product risk, increase testing productivity (efficiency), benchmark against an internationally-used model, and increasing the prestige of testing teams. Most survey respondents reported observing those benefits after adopting TMMi. Thus, most organizations have achieved the objectives they set when starting to do a TMMi based test process improvement project. This is confirmed by the high satisfaction ratio from the user survey. In answering the survey question, *"In general, have the TMMi-based test process improvement efforts been successful?"*, 87% of respondents stated that TMMi fully meets or exceeds their expectations; they are either satisfied, very satisfied, or extremely satisfied with benefits achieved or exceeded.

References

1. Garousi, V., Felderer, M., Hacaloğlu, T.: What we know about software test maturity and test process improvement. IEEE Softw. **35**(1), 84–92 (2018)
2. Gelperin, D., Hetzel, B.: The growth of software testing. Commun. ACM **31**(6), 687–695 (1988)
3. Burnstein, I., Homyen, A., Grom, R., Carlson, C.R.: A model to assess testing process maturity. Crosstalk J. Defense Softw. Eng. **11**, 26–30 (1998)
4. TMMi Foundation: TMMi specification (reference model), release 1.0 (2012)
5. TMMi Foundation: TMMi specification (reference model), release 1.2 (2018)

6. van Veenendaal, E., Shang, C., Xu, Y.: Achieving TMMi Level 3 – a Chinese case study. Qual. Matters Mag. **8**, 18–21 (2019)
7. Rungi, K., Matulevičius, R.: Empirical analysis of the Test Maturity Model Integration (TMMi). In: Skersys, T., Butleris, R., Butkiene, R. (eds.) ICIST 2013. CCIS, vol. 403, pp. 376–391. Springer, Heidelberg (2013). https://doi.org/10.1007/978-3-642-41947-8_32
8. Garousi, V., van Veenendaal, E.: Test Maturity Model integration (TMMi): trends of worldwide test maturity and certifications. IEEE Softw. **39**(2), 71–79 (2022)

AI in Software Engineering

Automated Code Review Comment Classification to Improve Modern Code Reviews

Miroslaw Ochodek[1]([✉]) [iD], Miroslaw Staron[2] [iD], Wilhelm Meding[3], and Ola Söder[4]

[1] Computer Science, Poznan University of Technology, Poznań, Poland
`miroslaw.ochodek@cs.put.poznan.pl`
[2] Computer Science and Engineering, Chalmers University of Gothenburg, Gothenburg, Sweden
`miroslaw.staron@gu.se`
[3] Ericsson AB, Stockholm, Sweden
`wilhelm.meding@ericsson.com`
[4] Axis Communications, Lund, Sweden
`ola.soder@axis.com`

Abstract. Modern Code Reviews (MCRs) are a widely-used quality assurance mechanism in continuous integration and deployment. Unfortunately, in medium and large projects, the number of changes that need to be integrated, and consequently the number of comments triggered during MCRs could be overwhelming. Therefore, there is a need for quickly recognizing which comments are concerning issues that need prompt attention to guide the focus of the code authors, reviewers, and quality managers. The goal of this study is to design a method for automated classification of review comments to identify the needed change faster and with higher accuracy. We conduct a Design Science Research study on three open-source systems. We designed a method (Comment-BERT) for automated classification of the code-review comments based on the BERT (Bidirectional Encoder Representations from Transformers) language model and a new taxonomy of comments. When applied to 2,672 comments from Wireshark, The Mono Framework, and Open Network Automation Platform (ONAP) projects, the method achieved accuracy, measured using Matthews Correlation Coefficient, of 0.46–0.82 (Wireshark), 0.12–0.8 (ONAP), and 0.48–0.85 (Mono). Based on the results, we conclude that the proposed method seems promising and could be potentially used to build machine-learning-based tools to support MCRs as long as there is a sufficient number of historical code-review comments to train the model.

Keywords: Modern Code Reviews · Machine learning · BERT

© Springer Nature Switzerland AG 2022
D. Mendez et al. (Eds.): SWQD 2022, LNBIP 439, pp. 23–40, 2022.
https://doi.org/10.1007/978-3-031-04115-0_3

1   Introduction

Modern Code Reviews [3] require a rapid response from the reviewers in order to facilitate short feedback loops and quick responses to the authors. Companies utilizing continuous integration, deployment, and delivery work actively to increase the speed of review and seek different methods to improve it [22]. Techniques used to speed up the review can vary, depending on the place in the review process, from automated recommendation of lines to review [18], automated reviewer recommendation [25], identification of refactoring possibilities [14] or attempts of automated code repairs [30].

However, in practice, during the phase of code review, performed using tools like Gerrit or GitHub, the review comments can vary in how specific they are, which hinders a quick identification of what should be improved in the code. Less specific comments, usually meant for long-term improvement of code, or even as a general discussion, can lead to slower development by postponing code integration. A discussion between code reviewer and code author, if they do not lead to a change, postpone the integration unnecessary and could be done outside of the system [24].

Leading roles in software development organizations, such as project managers, quality managers or measurement program leaders, continuously seek for improvements of the ways of working. Their responsibilities, however, do not provide them with the possibility to read and analyze all comments in the code review databases as the comments are meant for software developers, not quality managers. Therefore, automated support and a taxonomy can greatly improve their work. Such a taxonomy, taken together with defect reports, is a very powerful tool for finding systematic improvements in the ways of working of modern companies, especially when the development is distributed or done in empowered software development teams.

At the same time, the ability to quickly identify what should be changed in the code can speed up the review process, as well as the integration and subsequent testing. A good classification of the requested change can also lead to structural improvements in software development projects. In our previous studies, we established that it is possible to pinpoint which lines should be manually reviewed by using sentiment analysis to classify comments [23]. We have also demonstrated that it is possible to train a machine learning classifier to find lines of code that violate a specific coding guideline, defined by architects and designers [18]. However, an open issue is how to pinpoint the potential solution given a review comment written in a free text in the context of continuous integration (i.e. modern code reviews). Therefore, in this paper, we set off to address the following research question:

How to automatically classify code review comments to determine the focus of the code revision to be made?

Our results are two-fold. First, we designed a taxonomy of the purpose of code review comments and, second, a BERT-based tool for automatic classification of new comments. We evaluated this method by applying it to three open-source projects: the Mono Framework, Wireshark, and Open Network

Automation Platform (ONAP)—with a sample of 2,672 code-review comments that were extracted and manually labeled. The results show that for the categories with many comments (over 50), the results are strong (MCC of over 0.68 and accuracy of 0.97). For the categories with a lower number of comments, the accuracy is visibly lower (the lowest observed MCC was equal to 0.12 for one of the categories with only 19 review comments).

The remaining of the paper is organized as follows. In Sect. 2, we present the most relevant related work for this study are relate our results to these works. In Sect. 3, we present the taxonomy of the review comments and the machine learning mode which can classify new comments. In Sect. 4, we present the design of the research to evaluate the taxonomy and the tool. Section 5 presents the results from the evaluation of our proposed method on the three open source projects. Section 6 discusses the results from the perspective of their applicability to summarize comments and consistency between projects. Finally, we present the conclusions in Sect. 7.

2   Related Work

The field of code reviews and their analysis has been active since the 1970s and several systematic reviews of this field exist, e.g. Wang et al. [29]. Initially, the research focused on manual code reviews in form of walk-throughs where an experienced software engineer reviewed the code of others. An interesting side result of the work was that the modern code review research was done on only a few open-source projects—Qt, OpenStack, and Android. This work identified the problem which we address in our work—supporting the classification of review comments. This classification is needed to accelerate the reviews and to perform root-cause analysis afterward.

A systematic review of literature about modern code reviews (MCRs), conducted by Davilla et al. [10], studied documented practices of modern code reviews. Among others, they have found that "the review feedback is perceived as valuable when it provides an opportunity to learn and improve the code," which we address in this paper. Thanks to our industrial collaborations, we found that providing a taxonomy of code review comments can support this learning and systematic root cause analyses. The systematic review by Davilla et al. proposed a taxonomy of code reviews (finding 7), which we considered in our study, but revised as we needed to use more fine-grained categories.

In a similar manner, Badampuri et al. [4] studied literature in the area of modern code review and found that the majority of solutions proposed in that area are related to motivation enhancement, support for collaborative code review. They have also found several studies in the area of using static analysis to identify problematic code fragments and to review them. In our work, we want to go one step further and increase the ability to "codify" the knowledge of collaborative code reviews.

Several articles discuss the impact of code reviews, for example [19] or [27] who discuss it from the developers' perspective. Code reviews can trigger refactorings, but they need to be specific in their intent, otherwise, a code review risks being considered as a discussion trigger. However, there are studies that acknowledge negative aspects of modern code reviews, e.g. design degradation [26], slipping security defects [20] or staff turnover [17]. Therefore, automated support for this manual activity is still needed.

The static analysis tools and techniques are found to be helpful in code reviews, as Balachandran established [5]. They became a de-facto standard in automated support of code quality checks in continuous integration [21]. However, the static analysis techniques are not meant for that purpose and therefore often result in many false-positives, i.e. warnings which do not need to be addressed directly.

We could also observe that there are specific studies on how to identify selected violations of coding guidelines using machine learning. [2] proposed to use Normalised Compression Distance to find potential string overflows, null pointer references, memory leaks, and incorrect API usage. [8] reported findings on using machine learning techniques to detect defects in C programs at Oracle. They concluded that the ML-based tools were not suitable replacements for static program analysis tools due to the low precision of the results.

3   CommentBERT – Classifying Code-Review Comments

We propose a taxonomy of the focus of code-review comments and build a machine-learning-based model that allows to automatically classify code comments according the proposed taxonomy. The goal of the taxonomy is to provide a structure to group similar comments – for root cause analysis – and link them to changes in the source code – for improving the speed of code reviews.

3.1   Classifying Comments According to Their Focus

Figure 1 presents the taxonomy of comments. The taxonomy was designed as a result of topic analysis of comments from the Wireshark project [9]. At first, one of the researchers analyzed 1,248 code-review comments and incrementally generated topics. The topics were used to label each of the comments. In the following steps, the initial version of the taxonomy (with some exemplary comments belonging to each of the categories) was discussed between the researchers. The code-review comments categories resulted from the analysis are non-exclusive. It means that one comment could be categorized into more than one category. It is important, as commenting can take very different forms and the goal of the taxonomy is to guide the authors and reviewers rather than finding the best, single, fit for the comment. Finally, another researcher used the resulting taxonomy to verify the labeling of the dataset. Any doubts on how to categorize particular comments were discussed by the researchers.

The categories of the taxonomy are as follows.

code_design – the comment is about a structural organization of code into modules, functions, classes, and similar, e.g. "code snippet inherited from original dissector. I have refactored the code to have the decompression in a single place

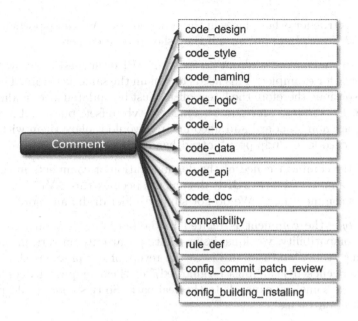

Fig. 1. Taxonomy of comments. Each review comment can be categorized to one or more categories.

now it should be a bit better". It is also about overriding, e.g. "this will not work for IA5. Why not simply override dataCoding before the switch?", and dead/unused code, e.g. "This is duplicated code, put outside the if-else.".

code_style – the comment is about the layout of the code, readability issues, for example: "add blank line" or "formatting: remove space after 4".

code_naming – the comment is about issues related to naming code constructs, tables, for example "please use lowercase for field name => 'isakmp.sak.nextpayload'" or "Add name of dissector XXX: use custom..."

code_logic – the comment is about algorithms used, operations on data, calling functions, creating objects, and also the order the operations are performed, for example "missing validation of chunk size, potential buffer overflow?" or "should this be initialized with NULL or something?"

code_io – the comment is about input/output, GUI, for example: "What about showing the hub port, i.e. 'address:port'? So the normal endpoints would display as 'address.endpoint' and split would display as 'address:port'" or "Debug output to be removed?".

code_data – the comment is about data, variables, tables, pieces of information, strings, for example: "You probably want encoding ENC_BIG_ENDIAN here. You could also use proto_tre_add_item-ret()int() here to avoid fetching the value twice. This is true for other places in the code too" or "Are these ports registered with IANA? If not, I am not sure if they should be used here".

code_api – the comment is about an existing API or suggestions how the API should evolve, for example: "This needs to remain the same as before. The dissection must continue therefore the latest offset must be updated after adding to the tree. offset += dissect_dsmcc_un_session_nsap(tvb, offset, pinfo, sub_sub_tree)" or "If they are non-standard and uncommon, I would replace them with: dissector_add_for_decode_as("udp.port", otrxd_handle)".

code_doc – the comment concerns the documentation or comments in the source code, for example: "Which 3GPP document specifies this AVP?" or "Maybe remove this comment now? We do not support older drafts anymore".

compatibility – the comment is related to the operating system's compatibility, tools' compatibility, versions, issues that appear only on certain platforms, for example: "the Ubuntu failure is to the revert of my previous change (only on_btnImport_clicked() call must be guarded)" or "I can empirically confirm that /proc/self/exe somehow expands to the real path. So this code would probably have no effect on Linux".

rule_def – the comment can be used to elicit a definition of coding/style rules, note it has to explain the broader context, e.g., "'add blank line' is not a definition since we don't know why the blank line should be added here; on contrary, 'use space for indent (like rest of file)' states that spaces should be used for indentation (in general)" or "remove comment when it doesn't help understanding the code".

config_commit_patch_review – the comment is about patches, commits, review comments, for example: "To be done in the next patch set" or "Right, if you decide to do a formatting patch, it is best to do that in a separate change".

config_building_installing – the comment is about a process of building, installing, and running the product, for example "This is not required. Already done by the install script" or "let's remove this example, installing binary packages across different distros is not supported and we should not recommend users to skip signature checking, etc.".

Naturally, this taxonomy can be used manually to understand and classify each comment, but the best support is to use an automated classifier of these comments. The classifier needs to be based on techniques from natural language processing and has to utilize a pre-trained model as the number of comments in a typical repository is not in parity to the diversity of the natural language constructs available.

3.2   Training BERT for Code-Review Comments

We based our classifier on the BERT (Bidirectional Encoder Representations from Transformers) language model [11], which is a deep artificial neural network based on a multi-layer bidirectional Transformer [28] (however, technically, it uses only the Transformer Encoder stack). The model is pre-trained on a large corpus of plain text for masked word prediction and next sentence prediction tasks. Such a base BERT model can be further trained to a specific downstream task.

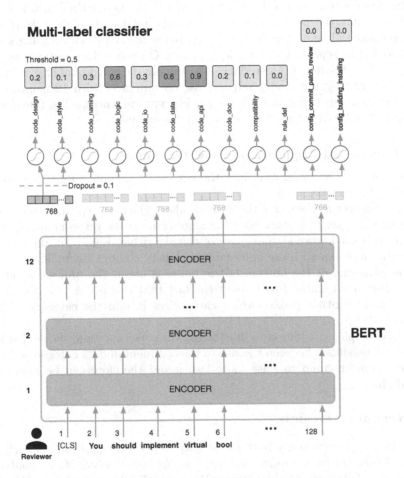

Fig. 2. CommentBERT architecture.

The architecture of our model, which we call CommentBERT is presented in Fig. 2[1]. There is a related model called CodeBERT model [12], however, it was

---

[1] https://github.com/mochodek/bertcomments.

trained using the pairs of class methods' code and their documentations what makes it specialized for so-called NLP-PL tasks, e.g., searching code fragments based on queries in a natural language, rather than a general-purpose usage).

The input to CommentBERT is a tokenized code-review comment. BERT uses a WordPiece tokenizer [32], which uses a fixed vocabulary to tokenize words in the text (an unknown word could be split into sub-words that are present in the vocabulary). We have set the input length to 128 tokens based on the analysis of the lengths of code-review comments.[2] Finally, BERT adds a special token [CLS] at the beginning of the input sequence.

The input is transformed by going through 12 layers of BERT encoders. Each encoder outputs the hidden state of 768 numbers for each of the tokens in the input sequence. The output for the [CLS] token has a special meaning since it is considered to represent the whole sequence. On top of that output, we build a multi-label classifier by introducing a dropout layer (probability = 0.1) to prevent overfitting the model and a dense output layer with 12 neurons—one per category in our taxonomy. We use the binary cross-entropy loss function and the sigmoid activation function for each of the outputs.

3.3 Example of Application of the Taxonomy

Figure 3 presents an example of how the taxonomy is applied for two comments from the Wireshark project.

The comment at the top of the figure is about the data type as it refers to the length of the type. It is also about the algorithm, as the reviewer suggests that the length is not known at that place of the algorithm. Finally, it also mentions a potential problem with the build failure, thus it is about the building process.

The comment at the bottom of the figure is about the process of building the product (compilation) and about the fact that this problem was addressed previously in another patch—which categorizes it into the category of patch review.

This example, in addition to illustrating the categorization, shows that there can be a dependency between the size of the comment and its categories. Longer review comments tend to raise more issues and therefore can be assigned to several classes.

4   Research Design

Since the goal of our study is to investigate *how to automatically classify code review comments to determine the focus of the code revision to be made?*, we are going to follow the Design Science Research (DSR) methodology [31]. DSR focuses on developing and evaluating artifacts and solutions for practical purposes. In particular, we focus on designing and validating the treatment (the CommentBERT model for classifying code-review comments according to the proposed taxonomy), which are two of the DSR-engineering-cycle steps.

---

[2] The input length of 128 tokens corresponds to the 98 percentile of the comment lengths distribution in the dataset of code reviews under study.

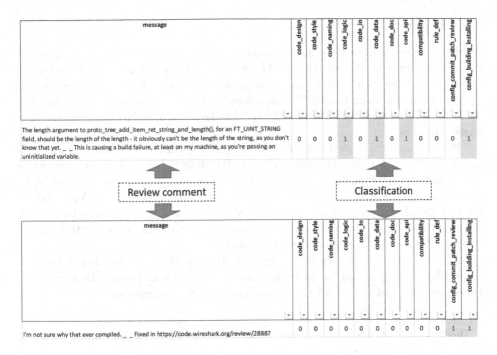

Fig. 3. An example classification of two comments.

4.1 Research Questions

We defined the following research questions that need to be answered to validate the CommentBERT model:

- RQ1: How accurate the CommentBERT model could be when classifying code-review comments according to the proposed taxonomy, assuming it is trained on and applied to the same project?
- RQ2: How accurate a pre-trained CommentBERT could be when applied cross-project?
- RQ3: How the accuracy of the CommentBERT is affected by the number of training examples?

RQ1 is a central research question of the validation study. We would like to investigate to what degree the CommentBERT model can be trained on and applied to classify code-review comments within the same project. In the second research question (RQ2), we would like to investigate the possibility of training and using the CommentBERT model cross-project. Finally, we would like to study the sensitivity of the CommentBERT to the number of positive examples in the training dataset (RQ3) since some of the categories in our taxonomy could be underrepresented in real-life code-review datasets. Therefore, we would like to learn what is the minimum number of positive instances in the training dataset to achieve reasonable accuracy of the model.

4.2   Datasets

Table 1 presents three free and open-source software (FOSS) projects selected for this study, i.e., Wireshark, ONAP, and the Mono Framework. We selected these projects as they were available as open-source, but they are actively developed and used commercially. The developers in the community have industrial affiliations, which indicates that software development standards are followed for these projects.

We randomly sampled code-review comments from Gerrit instances (Wireshark and ONAP) and GitHub (Mono). We manually labeled the comments according to the proposed taxonomy. At this stage our dataset consisted of 2,672 comments (Wireshark = 1,248, ONAP = 1,252, and Mono = 172). We observed that some of the comments were duplicated, however, they regarded different lines of code. Therefore, they represent a natural reviewers' tendency to respond in a similar way to similar issues in the code.

The code-review comments from ONAP and Mono were labeled by two researchers using a similar procedure as for Wireshark. During that process, there was no need to extend the taxonomy with new categories.

Table 1. The sample of code-review comments from FOSS projects under study.

Project	#Comments	Description
Wireshark	1248	Wireshark is a protocol analyzer, written mostly in C and maintained by constributors from several companies
ONAP	1252	ONAP (Open Network Automation Platform) is a platform for orchestration, management, and automation of network and edge computing services
Mono	172	The Mono Framework is a Linux implementation of the Microsoft .NET framework

4.3   Model Validation

To answer RQ1, we perform 10 runs of 10-fold cross-validation for each of the datasets. For each fold, we fine-tune the BERT model and set the batch size to fully utilize the memory. We use the RAdam optimizer with $\beta1 = 0.9$, $\beta2 = 0.999$, the base learning rate set to 1e−4, and perform 15 epochs of training. We use the same hyperparameters for RQ2, however, this time we train the model using the two datasets and apply it to classify code-review comments in the remaining one. Finally, we investigate the accuracy of the model for different types of categories and juxtapose it with the frequency of appearance of the comments belonging to these categories in the datasets to discuss RQ3.

We base the analysis of the results on three well-recognized prediction quality measures: accuracy, Matthews Correlation Coefficient (MCC), and area under the receiver operating characteristic (ROC) curve (AUC). Accuracy is the ratio between the correctly classified comments and all comments. Although the measure is straightforward to interpret, it is also very sensitive to a class imbalance in the datasets. MCC is a variant of Pearson's correlation coefficient for binary classification (it takes values from -1 to 1). It can be used to evaluate prediction quality for imbalanced datasets [6] and is also recommended for the evaluation of machine learning algorithms in software engineering [15]. We use the thresholds provided by Akoglu [1] to interpret the effect size based on MCC in our study. Finally, the last measure in our suite is AUC. It is based on ROC curve, which shows the level of balance between recall and precision. AUC takes values from 0 to 1, where 0 indicates a perfectly inaccurate model and a value of 1 reflects a perfectly accurate one. In general, an AUC of 0.5 suggests no discrimination, 0.7 to 0.8 is considered acceptable, 0.8 to 0.9 is considered excellent, and more than 0.9 is considered outstanding [16].

5   Results

The results of the cross-validation procedure are presented in Table 2 (Wireshark), Table 3 (ONAP), and Table 4 (Mono). We excluded categories with less than 10 comments to consider only the cases when, at least statistically, there would be at least one comment belonging to a given category in each fold while executing the cross-validation procedure.

The accuracy of the trained models ranged from 0.84 to 0.99 (mean = 0.94). Such high accuracy can be attributed to the class imbalance in the datasets. The average MCC value was equal to 0.60 which can be considered as of moderate to strong correlation [1]. Finally, the average AUC was equal to 0.76, which is considered acceptable [16]. Of course, the results differ depending on the category and dataset. The most consistent results (MCCs within 0.10) were obtained for code_io, code_style, code_data, rule_def, and code_logic categories. The results differed the most for code_doc and compatibility (MCC ranged between 0.29 and 0.42, respectively). The MCC ranged within 0.20 for the remaining categories.

The results for the cross-project application of the CommentBERT model are presented in Table 5. The prediction quality of such models was lower than in the case of intra-project training and application. However, for at least half of the categories, the MCCs could be interpreted as indicating at least fair to strong correlation. The best accuracy was achieved for the categories regarding coding style, logic, and data (MCC > 0.5). On contrary, the models struggled with recognizing comments regarding design issues, documentation, and input/output (MCCs < 0.10).

The results show that the number of examples in the training datasets seems to have a visible impact on the accuracy of the CommentBERT model.

Figure 4 presents how MCC, AUC, and their variability changes when the number of training examples increases. We observed a major improvement in both MCC and AUC for the categories having 20 or more instances in the

Table 2. Wireshark – the results of 10 × 10-fold cross-validation (ES – effect size, N–Negligible, P–Poor, W–Weak, F–Fair, M–Moderate, S–Strong, VS–Very Strong).

Category	n	Accuracy	MCC	ES (MCC) [1]	AUC	ES (AUC) [16]
code_design	44	0.98 (±0.00)	0.63 (±0.04)	M-S	0.72 (±0.01)	Acceptable
code_style	90	0.98 (±0.00)	0.82 (±0.02)	S-VS	0.88 (±0.01)	Excellent
code_naming	40	0.98 (±0.00)	0.54 (±0.04)	F-S	0.69 (±0.03)	Low
code_logic	397	0.85 (±0.01)	0.65 (±0.01)	M-S	0.83 (±0.01)	Excellent
code_io	41	0.97 (±0.00)	0.46 (±0.04)	F-S	0.66 (±0.03)	Low
code_data	486	0.86 (±0.01)	0.71 (±0.01)	M-VS	0.86 (±0.01)	Excellent
code_doc	50	0.96 (±0.00)	0.38 (±0.07)	W-M	0.64 (±0.03)	Low
code_api	148	0.93 (±0.00)	0.65 (±0.03)	M-S	0.81 (±0.02)	Excellent
compatibility	59	0.96 (±0.00)	0.54 (±0.04)	F-S	0.74 (±0.03)	Acceptable
rule_def	34	0.98 (±0.00)	0.43 (±0.05)	F-S	0.65 (±0.03)	Low
...patch_review	61	0.98 (±0.00)	0.72 (±0.02)	M-VS	0.82 (±0.01)	Excellent
...installing	53	0.96 (±0.00)	0.49 (±0.06)	F-S	0.71 (±0.03)	Acceptable

dataset. Also, the prediction quality becomes more stable when there are more training examples—a drop in standard deviations was observed when the size of training datasets increased.

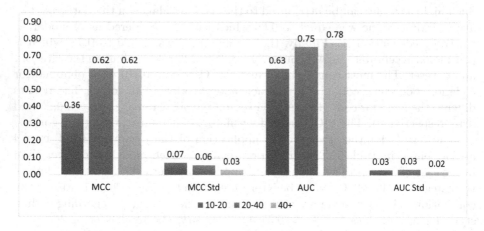

Fig. 4. Prediction quality of the models depending on the number of comments in categories (10–20, 20–40, and 40+).

Table 3. ONAP – the results of 10 × 10-fold cross-validation (ES – effect size, N–Negligible, P–Poor, W–Weak, F–Fair, M–Moderate, S–Strong, VS–Very Strong).

Category	n	Accuracy	MCC	ES (MCC) [1]	AUC	ES (AUC) [16]
code_design	98	0.93 (±0.00)	0.46 (±0.03)	F-S	0.69 (±0.02)	Low
code_style	109	0.97 (±0.00)	0.80 (±0.02)	S-VS	0.87 (±0.02)	Excellent
code_naming	49	0.98 (±0.00)	0.68 (±0.03)	M-S	0.79 (±0.03)	Acceptable
code_logic	471	0.86 (±0.01)	0.70 (±0.01)	M-S	0.85 (±0.01)	Excellent
code_io	18	0.99 (±0.00)	0.48 (±0.06)	F-S	0.67 (±0.03)	Low
code_data	333	0.87 (±0.00)	0.67 (±0.01)	M-S	0.83 (±0.01)	Excellent
code_doc	75	0.97 (±0.00)	0.68 (±0.02)	M-S	0.79 (±0.02)	Acceptable
code_api	121	0.94 (±0.00)	0.67 (±0.02)	M-S	0.82 (±0.02)	Excellent
compatibility	19	0.98 (±0.00)	0.12 (±0.08)	N-P	0.53 (±0.02)	Low
rule_def	43	0.97 (±0.00)	0.49 (±0.05)	F-S	0.69 (±0.03)	Low
...patch_review	37	0.98 (±0.00)	0.59 (±0.08)	F-S	0.73 (±0.04)	Acceptable
...installing	59	0.97 (±0.00)	0.63 (±0.02)	M-S	0.79 (±0.02)	Acceptable

Table 4. Mono – the results of 10 × 10-fold cross-validation for categories with ten or more examples (ES – effect size, N–Negligible, P–Poor, W–Weak, F–Fair, M–Moderate, S–Strong, VS–Very Strong)

Category	n	Accuracy	MCC	ES (MCC) [1]	AUC	ES (AUC) [16]
code_style	22	0.97 (±0.01)	0.85 (±0.04)	S-VS	0.89 (±0.03)	Excellent
code_logic	99	0.86 (±0.01)	0.71 (±0.03)	M-VS	0.85 (±0.01)	Excellent
code_data	67	0.84 (±0.02)	0.66 (±0.03)	M-S	0.83 (±0.02)	Excellent
code_api	16	0.93 (±0.01)	0.48 (±0.07)	F-S	0.67 (±0.04)	Low

6   Discussion

Classifying a single comment is useful, but having the taxonomy, and the automated tools for its application, provides us with the possibility to analyze all comments for the projects. Figure 5 shows a summary of the percentage of comments per category, grouped by the analyzed project.

Two of the categories are consistently the most frequent ones – comments about the logic of the program and comments about the data. This indicates that the reviewers discuss the algorithms, solutions to the problems rather than focusing on more "mundane" comment categories like the naming conventions or documentation of the code. Since these results are similar across the three analyzed projects, it indicates that the reviews are done for the same reasons in the studied projects. It can also indicate that the mechanisms for automated code analysis, like the static analysis tools, handle the simpler cases like naming conventions or documentation of the code (which are often regarded as technical debt [7, 13]).

On the other hand, the categories with the lowest percentage of classified comments, like the I/O category, could be connected to automated checking

Table 5. Prediction quality for cross-project model application (the mean values sorted by MCC in descending order).

Category	Accuracy	MCC	AUC
code_style	0.95	0.69	0.82
code_logic	0.80	0.58	0.79
code_data	0.81	0.56	0.77
code_api	0.91	0.48	0.72
config_commit_patch_review	0.97	0.46	0.65
code_naming	0.97	0.45	0.65
rule_def	0.98	0.31	0.57
compatibility	0.97	0.26	0.60
config_building_installing	0.96	0.25	0.57
code_design	0.94	0.08	0.53
code_doc	0.95	0.04	0.51
code_io	0.98	0.00	0.50

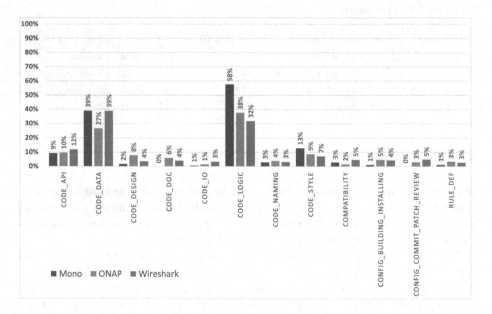

Fig. 5. Percentage of comments per category grouped by project.

tools. Our hypothesis, for further investigation, is that these kind of comments are only used when the proper I/O is used, but could be improved.

Finally, an interesting observation is the low frequency of the code-review comments belonging to the category of rule definition. To some extent, we expected more comments to relate to universal principles of writing code, e.g.

"use `AssertTrue(...)` instead of `AssertEqual(...)`". We based our expectation on the fact that there are guidebooks and coding guidelines for all projects, e.g. there exist one for Wireshark.[3]

When it comes to cross-project usage of the CommentBERT model, we observed that it is possible only to some degree. Our projects under study differ visibly when it comes to programming language, type of application, and architecture, therefore, the observed difficulties in cross-application of the model trained on different projects is not surprising. However, since the results were consistent for some of the categories, a potentially feasible solution would be to first fine-tune CommentBERT on open-source projects (since their code-review comments are easily accessible) and then continue training on a sample of code-review comments from a given project.

From the industrial perspective, leading roles, e.g., in line and projects, strive to continuously improve the ways of working in different areas. For this, they need to have tools that can effectively highlight pain-points. The CommentBERT can do that, if used properly. When a quality manager analyses the outcome of it over a year, for a product and/or team/-s, different patterns emerge quite soon. An example is which (of the 12) review areas are being commented frequently, and which seldom. Now, put that together with defect reports and test failures – interesting conclusions can be drawn:

- Comments about complex code_logic may be an indicator as to why it takes long time to find errors in the code or why the defect inflow is high. All customer errors reported are tied to how long time we have to fix them (depending on their severity) – if the time is not kept, we have to pay penalties
- Fast, successful integration is the goal of every software organization. Many comments on config_building_installing may indicate why the team fails to improve building and integration time.
- Errors in the code sometimes relate to backwards compatibility. These are difficult to find – but if CommentBERT has pointed out this repeatedly, then we can use it start scrutinizing the legacy parts instead of searching far and wide
- Another similar example are implicit dependencies – frequent comments on code_io and code_api may suggest this.

Based on the above observations, we could conclude that the proposed taxonomy and CommentBERT can form an important toolkit for quality managers in modern software development organizations.

The dataset and the models trained in our study can be used as a starting point to train comments' classification models for other open-source or industrial projects. The source code provided in the replication package for that study might constitute a baseline for training inter-project classifiers and building ML-based tools to be incorporated into CI pipelines.

---

[3] https://www.wireshark.org/docs/wsdg_html/.

7 Conclusions

Modern Code Reviews promise shorter feedback loops and faster delivery of higher quality code. However, they can also be a factor that decreases the speed of development—instead of improving the source code, programmers can get stuck in resolving misunderstandings.

In this study, we presented a method for automatically classifying review comments based on a taxonomy of what should be improved in the code. This method helps the designers to focus on the improvement potential suggested in the comments by the reviewers. Our proposed method uses machine learning for the automated classification of comments and it has been evaluated in three open-source projects. The results show that the accuracy is satisfactory, although it could be improved for these categories which are used sparsely.

Finally, when summarizing the results per category, we found that the programmers tend to discuss improvements in the usage of data types and designing the algorithms, rather than improving the visual appearance of the code or suggesting new coding guidelines.

In our future work, we plan to link the comments to the code which was commented, to find patterns that can be used to guide refactorings. For example, to be used to find the best match for methods to be used in program repair [14,30]. We also plan for a larger evaluation of our technique at our partner companies, including a longitudinal study of the improvements made to the source code based on these reviews.

References

1. Akoglu, H.: User's guide to correlation coefficients. Turk. J. Emerg. Med. **18**(3), 91–93 (2018)
2. Axelsson, S., Baca, D., Feldt, R., Sidlauskas, D., Kacan, D.: Detecting defects with an interactive code review tool based on visualisation and machine learning. In: The 21st International Conference on Software Engineering and Knowledge Engineering (SEKE 2009) (2009)
3. Bacchelli, A., Bird, C.: Expectations, outcomes, and challenges of modern code review. In: 2013 35th International Conference on Software Engineering (ICSE), pp. 712–721. IEEE (2013)
4. Badampudi, D., Britto, R., Unterkalmsteiner, M.: Modern code reviews-preliminary results of a systematic mapping study. In: Proceedings of the Evaluation and Assessment on Software Engineering, pp. 340–345. ACM (2019)
5. Balachandran, V.: Reducing human effort and improving quality in peer code reviews using automatic static analysis and reviewer recommendation. In: Proceedings of the 2013 International Conference on Software Engineering, pp. 931–940. IEEE Press (2013)
6. Boughorbel, S., Jarray, F., El-Anbari, M.: Optimal classifier for imbalanced data using matthews correlation coefficient metric. PLoS ONE **12**(6), 1–17 (2017). https://doi.org/10.1371/journal.pone.0177678
7. del Carpio, P.M.: Identification of architectural technical debt: an analysis based on naming patterns. In: 2016 8th Euro American Conference on Telematics and Information Systems (EATIS), pp. 1–8. IEEE (2016)

8. Chappelly, T., Cifuentes, C., Krishnan, P., Gevay, S.: Machine learning for finding bugs: an initial report. In: IEEE Workshop on Machine Learning Techniques for Software Quality Evaluation (MaLTeSQuE), pp. 21–26. IEEE (2017)
9. Cruzes, D.S., Dyba, T.: Recommended steps for thematic synthesis in software engineering. In: 2011 International Symposium on Empirical Software Engineering and Measurement, pp. 275–284. IEEE (2011)
10. Davila, N., Nunes, I.: A systematic literature review and taxonomy of modern code review. J. Syst. Softw. **177**, 110951 (2021)
11. Devlin, J., Chang, M.W., Lee, K., Toutanova, K.: Bert: pre-training of deep bidirectional transformers for language understanding. arXiv preprint arXiv:1810.04805 (2018)
12. Feng, Z., et al.: Codebert: a pre-trained model for programming and natural languages. arXiv preprint arXiv:2002.08155 (2020)
13. de Freitas Farias, M.A., Santos, J.A., Kalinowski, M., Mendonça, M., Spínola, R.O.: Investigating the identification of technical debt through code comment analysis. In: Hammoudi, S., Maciaszek, L.A., Missikoff, M.M., Camp, O., Cordeiro, J. (eds.) ICEIS 2016. LNBIP, vol. 291, pp. 284–309. Springer, Cham (2017). https://doi.org/10.1007/978-3-319-62386-3_14
14. Ge, X., Sarkar, S., Witschey, J., Murphy-Hill, E.: Refactoring-aware code review. In: 2017 IEEE Symposium on Visual Languages and Human-Centric Computing (VL/HCC), pp. 71–79. IEEE (2017)
15. Kitchenham, B.A., Pickard, L.M., MacDonell, S.G., Shepperd, M.J.: What accuracy statistics really measure. IEE Proc.-Softw. **148**(3), 81–85 (2001)
16. Mandrekar, J.N.: Receiver operating characteristic curve in diagnostic test assessment. J. Thorac. Oncol. **5**(9), 1315–1316 (2010)
17. Mirsaeedi, E., Rigby, P.C.: Mitigating turnover with code review recommendation: balancing expertise, workload, and knowledge distribution. In: Proceedings of the ACM/IEEE 42nd International Conference on Software Engineering, pp. 1183–1195 (2020)
18. Ochodek, M., Hebig, R., Meding, W., Frost, G., Staron, M.: Recognizing lines of code violating company-specific coding guidelines using machine learning. Empir. Softw. Eng. **25**(1), 220–265 (2019). https://doi.org/10.1007/s10664-019-09769-8
19. Paixão, M., et al.: Behind the intents: an in-depth empirical study on software refactoring in modern code review. In: Proceedings of the 17th International Conference on Mining Software Repositories, pp. 125–136 (2020)
20. Paul, R., Turzo, A.K., Bosu, A.: Why security defects go unnoticed during code reviews? A case-control study of the chromium OS project. In: 2021 IEEE/ACM 43rd International Conference on Software Engineering (ICSE), pp. 1373–1385. IEEE (2021)
21. Sadowski, C., Aftandilian, E., Eagle, A., Miller-Cushon, L., Jaspan, C.: Lessons from building static analysis tools at google (2018)
22. Staron, M., Meding, W., Söder, O., Bäck, M.: Measurement and impact factors of speed of reviews and integration in continuous software engineering. Found. Comput. Decis. Sci. **43**(4), 281–303 (2018)
23. Staron, M., Ochodek, M., Meding, W., Söder, O.: Using machine learning to identify code fragments for manual review. In: 2020 46th Euromicro Conference on Software Engineering and Advanced Applications (SEAA), pp. 513–516. IEEE (2020)
24. Thongtanunam, P., McIntosh, S., Hassan, A.E., Iida, H.: Review participation in modern code review. Empir. Softw. Eng. **22**(2), 768–817 (2016). https://doi.org/10.1007/s10664-016-9452-6

25. Thongtanunam, P., Tantithamthavorn, C., Kula, R.G., Yoshida, N., Iida, H., Matsumoto, K.I.: Who should review my code? A file location-based code-reviewer recommendation approach for modern code review. In: 2015 IEEE 22nd International Conference on Software Analysis, Evolution, and Reengineering (SANER), pp. 141–150. IEEE (2015)

26. Uchôa, A., et al.: How does modern code review impact software design degradation? An in-depth empirical study. In: 2020 IEEE International Conference on Software Maintenance and Evolution (ICSME), pp. 511–522. IEEE (2020)

27. Vassallo, C., Panichella, S., Palomba, F., Proksch, S., Gall, H.C., Zaidman, A.: How developers engage with static analysis tools in different contexts. Empir. Softw. Eng. **25**(2), 1419–1457 (2019). https://doi.org/10.1007/s10664-019-09750-5

28. Vaswani, A., et al.: Attention is all you need. arXiv preprint arXiv:1706.03762 (2017)

29. Wang, D., Ueda, Y., Kula, R.G., Ishio, T., Matsumoto, K.: The evolution of code review research: a systematic mapping study (2019)

30. Wen, F., Aghajani, E., Nagy, C., Lanza, M., Bavota, G.: Siri, write the next method. In: 2021 IEEE/ACM 43rd International Conference on Software Engineering (ICSE), pp. 138–149. IEEE (2021)

31. Wieringa, R.J.: Design Science Methodology for Information Systems and Software Engineering. Springer, Cham (2014). https://doi.org/10.1007/978-3-662-43839-8

32. Wu, Y., et al.: Google's neural machine translation system: Bridging the gap between human and machine translation. arXiv preprint arXiv:1609.08144 (2016)

A Preliminary Study on Using Text- and Image-Based Machine Learning to Predict Software Maintainability

Markus Schnappinger[1(✉)], Simon Zachau[1], Arnaud Fietzke[2],
and Alexander Pretschner[1]

[1] Technical University of Munich, Munich, Germany
{markus.schnappinger,simon.zachau,alexander.pretschner}@tum.de
[2] itestra GmbH, Munich, Germany
fietzke@itestra.de

Abstract. Machine learning has emerged as a useful tool to aid software quality control. It can support identifying problematic code snippets or predicting maintenance efforts. The majority of these frameworks rely on code metrics as input.

However, evidence suggests great potential for text- and image-based approaches to predict code quality as well. Using a manually labeled dataset, this preliminary study examines the use of five text- and two image-based algorithms to predict the readability, understandability, and complexity of source code.

While the overall performance can still be improved, we find Support Vector Machines (SVM) outperform sophisticated text transformer models and image-based neural networks. Furthermore, text-based SVMs tend to perform well on predicting readability and understandability of code, while image-based SVMs can predict code complexity more accurately.

Our study both shows the potential of text- and image-based algorithms for software quality prediction and outlines their weaknesses as a starting point for further research.

Keywords: Software maintainability · Expert judgment · Maintainability prediction · Machine learning · Text classification · Image classification

1 Motivation

With the rise of software, the assessment and improvement of its quality is an increasingly vital challenge. To support software quality control, a variety of automated tools and measurements exist. Still, some quality attributes are hard to determine without manual reviews [44]. As human analysts are expensive, predicting such properties with machine learning drew attention over the past

---

Both Simon Zachau and Markus Schnappinger should be considered main authors.

D. Mendez et al. (Eds.): SWQD 2022, LNBIP 439, pp. 41–60, 2022.
https://doi.org/10.1007/978-3-031-04115-0_4

years. For instance, it has successfully been applied to identify code smells [10, 13,33], support fault localization [48], and predict the maintainability of source code [42] or code changes [23,27].

Most contemporary studies rely on static code metrics as proxies for the actual source code. However, as Ray et al. [37] and Hindle et al. [19] point out, source code and natural language share certain characteristics, too. Accordingly, techniques originally designed for natural language have successfully been applied to source code, e.g. to aid recovery attacks against obfuscated programs [39], predict bugs [19], or identify code smells [32].

Hence, we hypothesize such algorithms can be employed for software quality prediction, too. Since readability and understandability are characteristics of both natural language and source code, we conjecture these attributes can be predicted particularly well using text-based machine learning.

Furthermore, there exists evidence that software analysts already build a strong hypothesis based on their first impression of the code. When analyzing and labeling the code used in this study, several experts confirmed they have been able to get an accurate intuition of the quality of a code snippet by looking at a visual representation of its overall structure, without going into syntactic or semantic detail. This applies in particular to assessments about the complexity and understandability of code. In this study, we try to mimic this process by training machine learning algorithms on images of source code. An example of such a visual representation is provided in Fig. 1.

Gap: Many researchers successfully applied machine learning on software metrics to predict software quality [17,23,27,35,43]. However, despite recent advances in text and image classification, these techniques are not used so far to predict software quality attributes as perceived by human experts.

Solution: This preliminary study explores the potential of two yet unapplied machine learning techniques for quality prediction. In this study, we conduct experiments in both a multi(4)-class and a binary classification setting. We compare the performance of five text-based and two image-based machine learning approaches using a publicly available, manually labeled dataset. The code is sampled from seven software projects and contains both open-source and proprietary projects. The learned quality label corresponds to the consensus of at least three analysts.

Contribution: Using text-based input, Support Vector Machines outperform other algorithms including Naive Bayes, BERT, RoBERTa, and CodeBERT by a large margin. Considering binary classification, they reach the same accuracy as an average human analyst. They are able to predict the readability, understandability, and complexity of source code with Matthews Correlation Coefficients (MCC) above 0.61 and F-Scores above 0.81, while a ZeroRule baseline classifier yields an MCC of 0.0 and F-Scores below 0.38. Furthermore, we observe better performance for binary classification than for ordinal multiclass prediction. While the naive baseline is outperformed by far in the first case, it is only slightly exceeded in the second case. This observation holds for both text-based

Fig. 1. First impressionistic, unreadable visualization of source code. The example on the left shows code that was later on considered hard to maintain, while the example on the right is rather easy to maintain. The examples feature the classes `Cells.java` and `UniformTexture.java`, resp., from *Art Of Illusion* [41].

and image-based algorithms. Here, image-based Support Vector Machines yield the best results as well with MCCs between 0.43 and 0.67 and F-Scores between 0.71 and 0.76.

These results are promising on the one hand, but are not yet applicable in practice on the other hand. Nevertheless, this preliminary study demonstrates the potential of image- and text-based classification algorithms for quality prediction and identifies which weaknesses remain to be addressed in further research. In particular, data preprocessing poses a major challenge.

Outline. The remainder of this paper is organized as follows. First, we describe in detail the experimental design including the dataset used, machine learning algorithms implemented, and data preprocessing techniques applied. Second, the experiment results are presented. This is followed by a critical discussion of the results and the limitations we identified. Eventually, we synthesize related research and alternative approaches to predicting software maintainability. The last chapter summarizes the study and presents our final conclusions.

2   Experimental Design

In this study, we examine the performance of text-based and image-based machine learning algorithms to predict the source code attributes readability, understandability, and complexity. Readability describes how easy it is for humans to syntactically parse written information [38]. In contrast, understandability is concerned with the ease of extracting relevant concepts and comprehending the semantics of a text or code snippet. Both attributes contribute significantly to software maintainability [1,47] and are also key characteristics of natural language texts. Hence, we investigate the use of classification algorithms from the natural language domain to predict these source code attributes.

Besides, the complexity of code has received lots of attention. The most popular approaches to capture the human intuition of code complexity are McCabe's cyclomatic complexity [30] and the cognitive complexity measure referred to by SonarQube [4]. While the effectiveness of these metrics is controversial, we observed human experts are able to build strong intuitions about code complexity even at first glance. This observation was made during the creation of the dataset described in Sect. 2.1. To recreate that first impression of an expert, we utilize images of source code. Then, we investigate the use of image classification to predict the complexity.

This section elaborates on the investigated algorithms, the used dataset, evaluation metrics, and preprocessing techniques.

2.1   Dataset

Unfortunately, there are only few software quality datasets publicly available. In 1993, Li and Henry [27] published a dataset containing the number of changed lines per code file. This attribute is often used as a proxy for software maintainability, e.g. in prediction experiments by [26,27,51]. However, that dataset does not distinguish between different maintainability aspects. Hence, there is no possibility to target specific sub-characteristics such as readability or complexity.

In contrast, we consider a manually labeled dataset that provides expert evaluations of the readability, understandability, perceived complexity, modularity, and overall maintainability of Java classes [40,41].

This dataset is a collection of code snippets from five open-source and four proprietary projects reviewed and rated by various experts. In total, 70 professionals participated in the creation of the dataset. The participants are affiliated with 17 different organizations including Airbus, Audi, BMW, Facebook, and Oracle. Eventually, the study was able to collect around 2,000 assessments, covering 519 Java classes.

Software quality consists of several sub-aspects such as maintainability or security [20]. Similarly, maintainability can also be divided into several sub-aspects. In our case, the assessment focuses on the sub-categories complexity, modularity, readability, and comprehensibility as well as the overall maintainability judgment of the expert. This decomposition guides the experts which viewpoints to consider during the assessment and mitigates the threat to construct validity, i.e. different participants might not share the same understanding of the broad term *maintainability*. Furthermore, this division enables researchers to focus on specific sub-aspects such as readability or comprehensibility.

Despite this decomposition into sub-characteristics and limited viewpoints, the subjective nature of the assessment remains problematic. Therefore, each class was evaluated by at least three experts. The Expectation-Maximization algorithm [8] finally aggregates their votes and computes the most probable 'true' label for each maintainability category. For more information about the selection of the study objects and the detailed labeling procedure please refer to [40] and [41].

In the presented machine learning experiments, we consider the aggregated consensus rating as the label. For our study, we have access to all open-source and two proprietary projects. The open-source dataset contains 304 entries, i.e. Java classes, which are extended to 374 entries by the two commercial projects. We conduct our experiments on both the open-source and extended versions to compare if the additional data makes a difference.

The experts labeled each code file on a four-part Likert scale, indicating whether they *fully agree, slightly agree, slightly disagree,* or *fully disagree* the code fulfills a certain quality attribute. This enables a fine-granular ordinal multiclass classification. In addition, we also examine a less fine-grained binary classification setting. Here, we separate the code into supposedly perfect (*strongly agree*) and not fully perfect code. Problematically, the dataset is imbalanced: Most code files are labeled as readable, understandable, and not complex, whereas very few entries are considered the opposite. This can lead to underrepresented labels getting only little attention during training and to distorted evaluation results. For the binary setting, the distribution is less imbalanced. The distributions for both settings are depicted in Table 1. The values in parentheses denote only the publicly available data.

2.2 Architectures and Algorithms

There are a plethora of machine learning architectures available. In the following, we explain the chosen algorithms in detail. Besides the text and image classification algorithms described below, we deploy Support Vector Machines (SVM) [5], which are capable of processing both texts and images.

Text-Based Learning. Naive Bayes [31] is a common classifier for text-based input. Here, a TF-IDF analysis preprocesses the text and determines how important specific terms in the analyzed text are. Furthermore, various transformer architectures have become prevalent in text-based machine learning use

Table 1. Distribution of the dataset in both the multiclass (top) and binary case (bottom). The values in parentheses denote the number of entries from open-source projects.

Multiclass label	Number of data points		
	Readability	Understandability	Complexity
Strongly agree	203 (183)	193 (157)	26 (22)
Weakly agree	111 (79)	96 (76)	51 (41)
Weakly disagree	47 (38)	60 (51)	75 (60)
Strongly disagree	13 (4)	25 (20)	222 (181)
Binary label			
Supp. perfect code	203 (183)	193 (157)	222 (181)
Other	171 (121)	181 (147)	152 (123)

cases. Hence, we employ BERT [9], CodeBERT [12], and RoBERTa [28] in this study, too.

While BERT, the Bidirectional Encoder Representations from Transformers, can suffer from unfortunate random initialization, RoBERTa (Robustly optimized BERT approach) is considered more stable [28]. CodeBERT, in contrast, was designed specifically to analyze source code and its connection to natural language [12]. Due to the small size of our dataset, we have resorted to pre-trained, publicly available models[1] and then fine-tuned them to the downstream task of maintainability prediction. For more information about these models please refer to [9,12,28].

Image-Based Learning. Convolutional neural networks are known to recognize specific features within images and classify images based on these structures. Due to external limitations of this study, we could not test all available neural network and deep learning setups. AlexNet [25] is a reasonable choice here since it consists of basic layers that integrate well with most machine learning frameworks. For the configuration of the network, we follow Karpathy et al. [22]. One challenge for convolutional neural networks, in general, is the need for a large training dataset.

---

[1] BERT: https://huggingface.co/bert-base-uncased.
RoBERTa: https://huggingface.co/roberta-base.
CodeBERT: https://huggingface.co/microsoft/codebert-base.

2.3   Training and Evaluation

Since the dataset is quite small, we dedicate 80% of the data for training and 20% for testing. This is a trade-off to accommodate both needs – a large enough training part for the training-intensive architectures, as well as a large enough testing part for evaluating and comparing the approaches. Using stratified splits accounts for equal label distributions in both partitions, thus mitigating the effects of the imbalanced label distribution. In contrast to related work [42], we shuffled the dataset before splitting and did not consider project boundaries.

During training, we applied grid-search cross-validation to identify the best performing hyper-parameters and internal preprocessing options. For the text-based approaches, we examined e.g. the use of stemming, camelCase splitting, and the number of tokens to be respected in n-grams. For the SVM architectures, we varied their internal kernels, namely Polynomial, Sigmoid and Radial Basis kernels.

Metrics to evaluate machine learning models are based on different perspectives on the confusion matrix. For multiclass classification, there are two ways to calculate performance scores: In macro-aggregation, the respective metric is applied to each class separately and aggregated afterward. Aggregating all classes before calculating the respective metrics is called micro-aggregation. In this study, we use micro-aggregation. In this case, F-Score, precision, recall, and accuracy yield identical values when evaluating multiclass predictions. For the remainder of this paper, we will thus only use F-Score to refer to this value. Due to the imbalance of the dataset, we consider the Matthews Correlation Coefficient (MCC) [14] as well. Its use is common and suggested in the defect prediction domain, where imbalanced data distributions are commonly observed [50]. The MCC measures the alignment of two raters while considering agreement might happen by chance. In our context, we consider the learned model the first rater, and the ground truth as the output of a second rater. A value equal to zero indicates random alignment, while a value of 1 indicates perfect alignment and a value of -1 corresponds to perfect inverse alignment.

To put the performance of all learned models into context, we establish two baselines. A naive ZeroRule classifier identifies the most common label in the training set and always predicts this label. Due to its constant nature, the MCC of this classifier is 0. Comparing the ratings of the individual human experts to the eventual consensus vote, we find frequent deviations between them. In fact, the average expert is only aligned with the consensus in approx. 63–70% of the cases, depending on the considered quality attribute. This human-level performance provides an illustrative, second baseline.

Both baselines are summarized in Table 2. For readability reasons, the table is restricted to performances on the extended dataset only. Please note the performance of the ZeroRule classifier depends on the data distribution. In our case, its values are identical for the binary and multiclass settings. This is because the most common class in the multiclass analysis is identical with the supposedly perfect code in the binary setting.

Table 2. Baselines for multi-class prediction and binary prediction

Multiclass baselines	Readability		Understand.		Complexity	
	MCC	F-Score	MCC	F-Score	MCC	F-Score
Average expert	0.451	0.658	0.440	0.633	0.511	0.703
ZeroRule classifier	0.000	0.543	0.000	0.516	0.000	0.594
Binary baselines						
Average expert	0.613	0.797	0.621	0.804	0.581	0.940
ZeroRule classifier	0.000	0.543	0.000	0.516	0.000	0.594

2.4 Preprocessing for Text-Based Prediction

Before we can use the labeled code files for machine learning, we have to prepro-
cess them. For the text-based analysis, the code files are parsed as raw text and
then tokenized. For the transformer models, we use their integrated tokenizers.
As such, the BERT model comes with its own tokenizer, as do the RoBERTa and
CodeBERT models. Since these transformer architectures only accept inputs of
a length shorter than 512 tokens, we have to split the file into multiple parts and
treat each part as a distinct data point if it originally contains more tokens [45].
Thus, the dataset size increases. Notably, the labels in our dataset have been
assigned to the whole Java class. After splitting the code, we assign the original
label to all its parts.

In contrast, for Naive Bayes and text-based SVM we could use the complete files. The necessary features are produced by a Term Frequency – Inverse
Document Frequency (TF-IDF) analysis of the code file.

2.5 Preprocessing for Image-Based Prediction

For the image-based analysis, we transform the code files into syntax-highlighted
images. We decided to add syntax-highlighting to i) ease the identification of relevant structures and ii) mimic an analyst opening the file in a code editor. The
same color theme is used for all images. First, we transform the Java files to
PDF files using `PDFCode`[2]. Second, these files are converted into PNG files of
680×680 pixels. This size ensures the color from the syntax-highlighting is still
visible although single characters might be no longer readable, depending on the
length of the code. Due to resource constraints, our implementation of AlexNet
downsizes the images to 224×224 pixels similar to the original AlexNet [25]. Our
experiments with higher resolution images have not led to significant improvements.

The code is positioned in the top center of each image. An example is provided
in Fig. 2. There, the code is unreadable by design.

---

[2] https://github.com/xincoder/PDFCode.

Fig. 2. Image of syntax-highlighted source code from `UniformTexture.java` from *Art Of Illusion* [41]

2.6 Experiment Execution

AlexNet is implemented on top of `Keras` [6], while BERT and its derivatives use `PyTorch` [11]. Naive Bayes and SVMs are based on `scikit-learn` [34].

We conducted every experiment using the extended dataset and using only the open-source data. This allows for analyzing the effect of additional data points and increases the reproducibility of our results for those without access to the confidential data. A replication package is publicly available on GitHub[3].

Every experiment was executed with different random seeds to mitigate the effects of random bias. We limited ourselves to two seeds as we did not find large differences between the runs. The reported values correspond to the average.

---

[3] https://github.com/simonzachau/SWQD-predict-software-maintainability.

3   Experiment Results

Table 3. Prediction results on the extended dataset and performance obtained on the open-source data in parentheses.

Multiclass classifier	Readability		Understandability		Complexity	
	MCC	F-Score	MCC	F-Score	MCC	F-Score
Naive Bayes	0.196 (0.038)	0.587 (0.607)	0.136 (0.112)	0.540 (0.533)	0.000 (0.000)	0.600 (0.590)
SVM (text-based)	**0.358** (0.398)	**0.640** (0.705)	**0.332** (0.301)	**0.613** (0.598)	**0.284** (0.241)	**0.633** (0.623)
BERT	0.032 (0.017)	0.306 (0.316)	0.023 (0.017)	0.276 (0.273)	0.005 (−0.038)	0.259 (0.232)
RoBERTa	0.013 (0.001)	0.290 (0.314)	0.010 (−0.001)	0.280 (0.262)	−0.013 (0.021)	0.240 (0.271)
CodeBERT	−0.009 (0.027)	0.274 (0.327)	0.004 (0.042)	0.263 (0.295)	−0.012 (0.021)	0.234 (0.269)
SVM (image-based)	**0.232** (0.470)	**0.580** (0.713)	**0.302** (0.427)	**0.580** (0.631)	**0.402** (0.337)	**0.673** (0.615)
AlexNet	0.000 (0.000)	0.293 (0.607)	0.000 (0.000)	0.113 (0.205)	0.000 (0.000)	0.600 (0.164)
Binary classifier						
Naive Bayes	0.555 (0.538)	0.780 (0.779)	0.521 (0.695)	0.760 (0.844)	0.464 (0.478)	0.747 (0.746)
SVM (text-based)	**0.609** (0.554)	**0.807** (0.787)	**0.660** (0.657)	**0.827** (0.820)	**0.637** (0.523)	**0.827** (0.771)
BERT	−0.013 (−0.042)	0.629 (0.568)	−0.029 (0.031)	0.646 (0.656)	0.027 (0.005)	0.585 (0.574)
RoBERTa	−0.001 (−0.017)	0.613 (0.600)	0.026 (0.035)	0.674 (0.697)	−0.050 (−0.015)	0.615 (0.608)
CodeBERT	0.028 (0.016)	0.627 (0.602)	0.036 (−0.002)	0.680 (0.646)	0.018 (0.032)	0.653 (0.645)
SVM (image-based)	**0.513** (0.565)	**0.760** (0.795)	**0.430** (0.530)	**0.713** (0.762)	**0.667** (0.495)	**0.840** (0.754)
AlexNet	0.000 (0.000)	0.453 (0.500)	0.006 (0.000)	0.500 (0.500)	0.000 (0.000)	0.400 (0.590)

For each classification approach, we investigate both the performance in a multi-class setting and a binary setting. The latter provides a first impression about the quality of the source code, while the multiclass prediction is more fine-grained. Table 3 lists the results concerning MCC and F-Score for each predicted quality attribute. The values in parentheses refer to the performance obtained using only the open-source data. The table shows the results for multiclass prediction in the top part, while the bottom part displays the results obtained for binary classification. Here, we combined three classes of the multiclass setting into one class as described in Sect. 2.1. To ease a comparison with the multiclass performance, we use F-Score and MCC to evaluate the binary prediction, too. Please note the micro-averaged F-Score yields the same value as the micro-averaged accuracy, precision, and recall scores.

3.1   Text-Based Classification

We find text-based SVMs outperform all other text-based approaches concerning MCC and F-Score independently of the predicted quality attribute. In the multiclass case, readability can be predicted with an MCC of 0.36 and F-Score of 0.64; understandability with an MCC of 0.33 and F-Score of 0.61; and complexity with an MCC of 0.28 and F-Score of 0.63. For binary predictions, an MCC of 0.61 and F-Score of 0.81 is reported for readability; 0.66 and 0.83 for understandability; and 0.64 and 0.83 for complexity.

The second-best classifier is Naive Bayes. It delivers the second-best results for readability and understandability. However, for the complexity label, its results are identical to the constant ZeroRule classifier. Notably, BERT, RoBERTa, and CodeBERT perform worse than the naive baseline classifier regarding the F-Score. Their MCC is close to 0 in all experiments, thus indicating only little information was learned during training.

In the binary setting, text-based SVMs outperform other text classification approaches as well. However, the difference to Naive Bayes is much smaller compared to the multiclass prediction. The obtained performance values are notably higher than in multiclass settings. The MCC is at 0.61, 0.66, and 0.64, resp.

3.2 Image-Based Classification

SVMs appear superior for image-based classification as well. AlexNet yields an MCC of 0 in all experiments, indicating the algorithm was not able to learn any relevant information and performed only as well as the constant classifier. Notably, its F-Score in the multiclass setting is even below the baseline for readability and understandability. In the binary case, AlexNet achieved F-Scores slightly above the baseline while the MCC remains at 0. In contrast, SVM obtained an MCC of 0.51 and F-Score of 0.76 for readability, 0.43 and 0.71, resp., for understandability, and 0.67 and 0.84 for complexity.

3.3 Interpretation

For an easier comparison of the seven approaches, we visualize the MCC obtained on the extended dataset in Fig. 3 (multiclass classification) and Fig. 4 (binary classification).

In our experiments, we found Naive Bayes and SVMs to perform better than convolutional neural networks and transformers. Further, we observe binary classification yields better results than multiclass prediction. On the extended dataset, the text-based approaches tend to perform better when predicting readability and understandability while the image-based approaches predict complexity more accurately. This is in line with our hypotheses.

Naive Bayes and SVMs perform better than expected, whereas AlexNet and the transformer approaches are below expectations. The SVM can play to its strengths of performing well on small datasets. At the same time, the small size of the dataset, as well as its imbalance, are likely to be the problem for convolutional neural networks and transformer architectures. Another evidence for this is that the interpretation of the dataset as binary classes almost exclusively achieved higher scores than in the multiclass scenario.

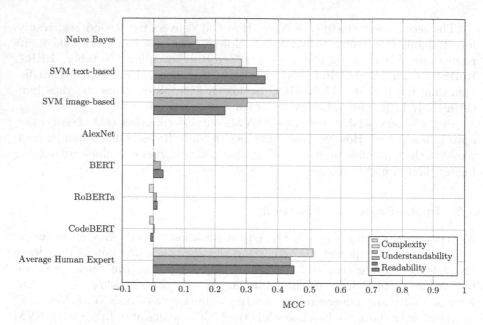

Fig. 3. Comparison of the MCC for multiclass classification

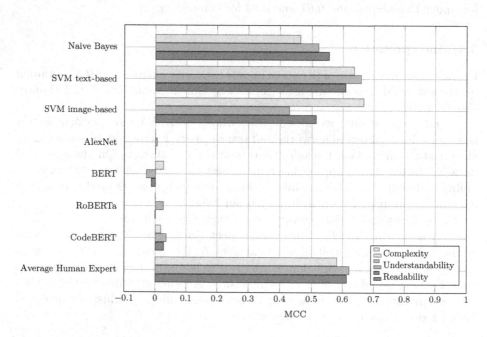

Fig. 4. Comparison of the MCC for binary classification

The transformer models BERT, RoBERTa, and CodeBERT achieve similar results in all experiments. However, the obtained MCC is close to 0. Thus, these models can be compared to randomly selecting a label. Still, all possible labels have been predicted at least once in our experiments.

Analyzing the predicted classes, we found some algorithms did not predict certain labels at all. For instance, Naive Bayes did only predict one out of four possible labels for complexity, and only two out of four labels for readability in the multiclass setting. In the binary interpretation, all labels are predicted at least once, which leads to higher scores. In our tests with AlexNet, always only one class is predicted in every experiment. This holds across both multiclass and binary prediction as well as across the extended and the open-source dataset. This renders the numbers unusable to compare to other approaches.

4   Discussion

The results are promising on the one hand, but also demonstrate room for improvement on the other hand. As of now, we observe large deviations in the ordinal multiclass prediction between the performance of the trained models and human performance. While the ZeroRule baseline is only slightly exceeded in this setting, it is outperformed by far in the binary setting. It is encouraging to see the performance of the text- and image-based SVM model even reaches the performance of an average human expert concerning the MCC. However, this binary setting probably oversimplifies a complex problem. Still, these results provide evidence on the potential of applying text and image classification algorithms to predict software quality.

The extended dataset contributes 70 additional data points. However, we cannot confirm that more available data leads to better results in general. For instance, text-based SVM yielded a higher MCC and higher F-Score predicting multiclass readability on the smaller dataset. The same observation is made using the image-based SVM to predict readability or understandability. Still, in most cases, better performance was observed using the extended dataset.

So far, we are not aware of other studies using image-based classification on source code. A summary of related work is presented in Sect. 5. Due to the recentness of the dataset we used, only few comparable experiments are available. The most comparable experiment is described in [42]. The authors focused on the *overall maintainability* judgment of the code instead of single quality attributes like readability or understandability. Their models are based on static code metrics. Besides, they apply a different validation technique respecting project boundaries, while we shuffled the dataset before splitting it. Thus, the experiment settings are too different to reasonably compare the results.

We found preprocessing to be an extensive challenge for both image-based and text-based inputs. Most image-based machine learning architectures require an input of quadratic and constant size. Source code neither has a defined length nor a quadratic layout. We chose an image size of 680×680 pixels, which is a reasonable trade-off between the high number of dimensions and the training time.

Another challenge is the layout of the image. Either the code is displayed as large as possible, or with normalized font size. We decided not to normalize due to large discrepancies in the length of the code files. The longest file in this dataset is 28 pages long (ISO A4 format). Had we chosen to scale the size according to this maximum value, the majority of the images would have appeared completely void. Since the algorithms try to recognize structural patterns, we chose to display these structures as prominently, i.e. large, as possible.

In the text-based experiments, the hyper-parameters about stemming and camelCase splitting did not lead to significant differences in the performance of the SVM and Naive Bayes classifiers.

In this experiment, BERT and its derivatives could not predict any quality attribute reliably. We attribute the poor performance of the transformer models mainly to one characteristic: the limited input length. As they accept only input smaller or equal to 512 tokens, we had to split most code files. This is a problem if the quality defects leading to a bad quality judgment are not evenly distributed across a Java class, which is a reasonable assumption. If the use of text-based machine learning for quality evaluation is to be moved forward, quality labels on the granularity of smaller code snippets are needed. However, manually labeling a sufficient amount of data points was out of scope for this study.

For image-based approaches, AlexNet always predicted one class and neglected all others. Contrary to expectations, that one class varied between experiment runs and was not always the majority class. Oftentimes, such behavior indicates a bug. To validate our setup, we replaced the images of one class with black dummy images to contrast the otherwise predominantly white images. In that experiment, the prediction achieved a perfect result ($MCC = 1$). This confirms the correctness of the implementation. We also conducted experiments using AlexNet with larger input images. However, it did not yield a noticeable difference. We hypothesize that the content of the images looks too similar for the convolutional neural network to identify useful characteristics.

4.1   Threats to Validity

The biggest threats to validity are introduced by the selected algorithms and used dataset. Though it is manually labeled and believed to contain the consensus of expert assessments, the dataset contains only a relatively small number of samples. Still, it is significantly larger than other, commonly used datasets such as the Li-Henry dataset [27]. However, the construct validity of manually labeled datasets is inherently threatened. Especially regarding software quality, which is deliberately defined vaguely [20,21], there exist several different viewpoints. We mitigated this threat by—instead of referring to the broad term software quality or maintainability—asking for evaluations with respect to more precise sub-attributes. In addition, the labeling platform offers explanations of the single attributes as tooltips. However, we recognize that participants may still interpret these terms differently.

As mentioned earlier, a large amount of machine learning algorithms exists. We made sure to include both simple (Naive Bayes and SVMs) and more sophisticated models such as transformers and neural networks. We acknowledge using more or different approaches may have led to different results. Due to the limitations of this study and the long training periods required by most approaches, we had to limit ourselves to a subset of all applicable algorithms. To mitigate the potential effects of random seeds, we performed each experiment twice and report the average. Though we did not find significant deviations between the runs, one could repeat the experiment several times more. Another threat is the bias introduced by the chosen train-test split, which we mitigated by shuffling and stratifying the data. While we are going to further improve these weaknesses in future experiments, we see value in this preliminary study and its results. To increase the reproducibility of our results, we report the performance of our classifiers on the publicly available dataset in Sect. 3 and provide a replication package.

4.2 Future Work

There are various ways of how to further improve our results and setup. Even the extended version of the used dataset is small compared to those typically used for image- or text-based learning. A larger and more balanced dataset can likely improve results for most of our approaches. The dataset at hand also admits a numerical interpretation of the labels. Hence, modeling the prediction as a regression model is an interesting possibility. In the future, we plan to analyze other machine learning architectures and incorporate techniques from Explainable Artificial Intelligence to foster the debugging and interpretation of the results.

5   Related Work

Automated software quality evaluation and control is an increasingly important topic. Lately, machine learning has been used to evaluate characteristics that typically need to be interpreted by human experts. This includes, e.g., maintainability prediction [17,27,43] or code smell detection [13,33]. An overview of machine learning techniques for code smell detection is provided in [10].

Text-based models for code have been utilized by Palomba et al. [32] to identify code smells based on textual analysis. Salem and Banescu [39] used the TF-IDF of source code to foster metadata recovery attacks on obfuscated source code. Corazza et al. [7] performed a study where they manually analyzed code comments and predicted human ratings using TF-IDF as well. Buse and Weimer [2,3] developed a metric for code readability based on entropy within the code. Their model was later refined by Posnett et al. [36]. While they do predict the readability of code, they use static measurements as features. In contrast, we use textual or image representations of the code.

To predict software maintainability, several related studies use a dataset published by Li and Henry [27], which refers to the number of changed lines as a proxy for maintainability. The data is drawn from only two software systems, which are programmed in Classic-ADA. Then, regression models are used to predict the number of changed lines [27]. Kaur and Kaur [23] summarize 27 experiments using this dataset. Furthermore, neuro-genetic algorithms were used by Kumar et al. [26], while van Koten and Gray applied Bayesian Networks [46].

Similar to these studies, Malhotra and Lata [29] use the observed changes in software systems as their target variable. Then, they discretize the data into binary classes corresponding to high and low maintainability. However, they do not provide the threshold used to separate them and mostly focus on the effects of data preprocessing techniques.

Another dataset for C programs was created in 1987 by Harrison and Cook [15]. This dataset is used for example by Xing et al. [49], who trained support vector machines on it, or by Khoshgoftaar et al. [24], who used regression models.

Other studies aim to predict the rating of human experts instead of code changes. Using the same dataset as in our study, the maintainability of code was predicted in [42]. Here, the authors employ a human-level baseline as well to put the performance of the evaluated machine learning classifiers into context. However, static code metrics are used as input and a different aspect of the dataset was chosen as the label. Hegedűs et al. [17] predicted the perceived changeability of methods using a three-fold label. They achieved an accuracy of 0.76, while the constant baseline classifier already yielded an accuracy of 0.67. On class-level, Schnappinger et al. [43] achieved an accuracy of 0.81, using a three-fold scale, too. Hayes and Zhao [16] used the perceived maintainability of software developed by students and developed a regression model to predict the judgment.

So far, we observe studies relying on human evaluations often do not report which maintainability sub-aspects the experts focused on [16,35,43], do not share their data publicly [43], or rely on the opinion of a single expert [16,18,35].

In this study, we target three fine-granular sub-dimensions of maintainability and evaluate classification techniques chosen specifically for these attributes. We explore the use of image and text classification algorithms to predict the readability, understandability, and complexity of source code.

6   Conclusion

Current machine learning approaches for predicting expert software quality evaluations often base their prediction on static code metrics. In related domains, image and text classification reached significant results as well, suggesting their potential use in quality prediction. In this study, we investigate how well *text-based* and *image-based* classification algorithms can predict readability, understandability, and complexity of code. We compare five text-based machine learning architectures (Naive Bayes, Support Vector Machines, BERT, RoBERTa, CodeBERT) and two image-based classifiers (Support Vector Machines, AlexNet). The labels are drawn from a publicly available, manually labeled dataset. We examine both a fine-granular ordinal multiclass classification and binary classification settings.

Using text-based input, Support Vector Machines outperform other algorithms by a large margin. In the binary classification setting, they are able to predict the readability, understandability, and complexity of source code with Matthews Correlation Coefficients above 0.61 and F-Scores above 0.81. Regarding image-based classification, Support Vector Machines yield the best results as well with F-Scores between 0.71 and 0.76. Although the employed models outperform a ZeroRule baseline classifier, the multiclass prediction does not yet reach an operational level. In contrast, in a simplified binary setting, our models reach human-level results. This demonstrates the potential of image and text classification algorithms.

However, in this preliminary study, we identified several open challenges for future research: In our view, the main challenge for the applicability of these approaches is currently posed by their need for fixed-size inputs. Indeed, state-of-the-art transformer models require text samples of fixed length. Similarly, most image-based algorithms assume a constant image size. This requires a preprocessing of source code files of unbounded length and arbitrarily complex structure into fixed-size data points, which in our experiments caused a deterioration of data quality. In particular, the partitioning of source code into fixed-length strings or fixed-size images did not match the granularity of the available labels.

This preliminary study opens an interesting line of research in quality prediction. As this was our first foray into using text- and image-based machine learning for software quality prediction, we are confident that subsequent work will improve on the identified limitations.

References

1. Banker, R.D., Datar, S.M., Kemerer, C.F., Zweig, D.: Software complexity and maintenance costs. Commun. ACM **36**(11), 81–95 (1993)
2. Buse, R., Weimer, W.: A metric for software readability. In: Proceedings of the 2008 International Symposium on Software Testing and Analysis, pp. 121–130. ACM (2008)
3. Buse, R., Weimer, W.: Learning a metric for code readability. IEEE Trans. Software Eng. **36**(4), 546–558 (2010)
4. Campbell, G.A.: Cognitive complexity: an overview and evaluation. In: Proceedings of the 2018 International Conference on Technical Debt, pp. 57–58 (2018)
5. Chang, Y.W., Hsieh, C.J., Chang, K.W., Ringgaard, M., Lin, C.J.: Training and testing low-degree polynomial data mappings via linear SVM. J. Mach. Learn. Res. **11**(48), 1471–1490 (2010)
6. Chollet, F.: Keras (2015). https://github.com/fchollet/keras
7. Corazza, A., Maggio, V., Scanniello, G.: Coherence of comments and method implementations: a dataset and an empirical investigation. Software Qual. J. **26**(2), 751–777 (2018)
8. Dempster, A.P., Laird, N.M., Rubin, D.B.: Maximum likelihood from incomplete data via the EM algorithm. J. Roy. Stat. Soc.: Ser. B (Methodol.) **39**(1), 1–22 (1977)
9. Devlin, J., Chang, M.W., Lee, K., Toutanova, K.: Bert: pre-training of deep bidirectional transformers for language understanding. In: Proceedings of the 2019 Conference of the North, pp. 4171–4186 (2019)

10. Di Nucci, D., Palomba, F., Tamburri, D.A., Serebrenik, A., De Lucia, A.: Detecting code smells using machine learning techniques: are we there yet? In: 2018 IEEE 25th International Conference on Software Analysis, Evolution and Reengineering (SANER), pp. 612–621. IEEE (2018)
11. Facebook: Pytorch (2020). https://pytorch.org
12. Feng, Z., et al.: CodeBERT: a pre-trained model for programming and natural languages. In: Findings of the Association for Computational Linguistics: EMNLP 2020. Association for Computational Linguistics, Online, November 2020
13. Fontana, F.A., Zanoni, M., Marino, A., Mäntylä, M.V.: Code smell detection: towards a machine learning-based approach. In: 2013 IEEE International Conference on Software Maintenance, pp. 396–399. IEEE (2013)
14. Gorodkin, J.: Comparing two k-category assignments by a k-category correlation coefficient. Comput. Biol. Chem. **28**, 367–374 (2004)
15. Harrison, W., Cook, C.: A micro/macro measure of software complexity. J. Syst. Softw. **7**(3), 213–219 (1987)
16. Hayes, J.H., Zhao, L.: Maintainability prediction: a regression analysis of measures of evolving systems. In: 21st IEEE International Conference on Software Maintenance (ICSM 2005), pp. 601–604. IEEE (2005)
17. Hegedűs, P., Bakota, T., Illés, L., Ladányi, G., Ferenc, R., Gyimóthy, T.: Source code metrics and maintainability: a case study. In: Kim, T., et al. (eds.) ASEA 2011. CCIS, vol. 257, pp. 272–284. Springer, Heidelberg (2011). https://doi.org/10.1007/978-3-642-27207-3_28
18. Hegedűs, P., Ladányi, G., Siket, I., Ferenc, R.: Towards building method level maintainability models based on expert evaluations. In: Kim, T., Ramos, C., Kim, H., Kiumi, A., Mohammed, S., Ślęzak, D. (eds.) ASEA 2012. CCIS, vol. 340, pp. 146–154. Springer, Heidelberg (2012). https://doi.org/10.1007/978-3-642-35267-6_19
19. Hindle, A., Barr, E.T., Gabel, M., Su, Z., Devanbu, P.: On the naturalness of software. Commun. ACM **59**(5), 122–131 (2016)
20. ISO/IEC: ISO/IEC 25010 - Systems and software engineering - Systems and software Quality Requirements and Evaluation (SQuaRE) - System and software quality models. Technical report (2010)
21. Jung, H.W., Kim, S.G., Chung, C.S.: Measuring software product quality: a survey of ISO/IEC 9126. IEEE Softw. **21**(5), 88–92 (2004)
22. Karpathy, A., Fei-Fei, L., Johnson, J.: Convolutional neural networks for visual recognition, Stanford University (2017). http://cs231n.github.io
23. Kaur, A., Kaur, K.: Statistical comparison of modelling methods for software maintainability prediction. Int. J. Software Eng. Knowl. Eng. **23**(06), 743–774 (2013)
24. Khoshgoftaar, T.M., Munson, J.C.: Predicting software development errors using software complexity metrics. IEEE J. Sel. Areas Commun. **8**(2), 253–261 (1990)
25. Krizhevsky, A., Sutskever, I., Hinton, G.E.: Imagenet classification with deep convolutional neural networks. Adv. Neural. Inf. Process. Syst. **25**, 1097–1105 (2012)
26. Kumar, L., Naik, D.K., Rath, S.K.: Validating the effectiveness of object-oriented metrics for predicting maintainability. Procedia Comput. Sci. **57**, 798–806 (2015)
27. Li, W., Henry, S.: Object-oriented metrics that predict maintainability. J. Syst. Softw. **23**(2), 111–122 (1993)
28. Liu, Y., et al.: Roberta: a robustly optimized bert pretraining approach. arXiv preprint arXiv:1907.11692 (2019)
29. Malhotra, R., Lata, K.: An empirical study on predictability of software maintainability using imbalanced data. Software Qual. J. **28**(4), 1581–1614 (2020)

30. McCabe, T.J.: A complexity measure. IEEE Trans. Software Eng. **4**, 308–320 (1976)

31. Murphy, K.: Naive Bayes classifiers. Univ. Br. Columbia **18**(60) (2006)

32. Palomba, F., Panichella, A., De Lucia, A., Oliveto, R., Zaidman, A.: A textual-based technique for smell detection. In: 2016 IEEE 24th International Conference on Program Comprehension (ICPC), pp. 1–10. IEEE (2016)

33. Pecorelli, F., Palomba, F., Di Nucci, D., De Lucia, A.: Comparing heuristic and machine learning approaches for metric-based code smell detection. In: 2019 IEEE/ACM 27th International Conference on Program Comprehension (ICPC), pp. 93–104. IEEE (2019)

34. Pedregosa, F., et al.: Scikit-learn: machine learning in Python. J. Mach. Learn. Res. **12**, 2825–2830 (2011)

35. Pizzi, N.J., Summers, A.R., Pedrycz, W.: Software quality prediction using median-adjusted class labels. In: Proceedings of the 2002 International Joint Conference on Neural Networks, IJCNN 2002, vol. 3, pp. 2405–2409. IEEE (2002)

36. Posnett, D., Hindle, A., Devanbu, P.: A simpler model of software readability. In: Proceedings of the 8th Working Conference on Mining Software Repositories, pp. 73–82. ACM (2011)

37. Ray, B., Hellendoorn, V., Godhane, S., Tu, Z., Bacchelli, A., Devanbu, P.: On the 'naturalness' of buggy code. In: 2016 IEEE/ACM 38th International Conference on Software Engineering (ICSE), pp. 428–439 (2016)

38. Raymond, D.R.: Reading source code. In: CASCON, vol. 91, pp. 3–16 (1991)

39. Salem, A., Banescu, S.: Metadata recovery from obfuscated programs using machine learning. In: Proceedings of the 6th Workshop on Software Security, Protection, and Reverse Engineering, pp. 1–11 (2016)

40. Schnappinger, M., Fietzke, A., Pretschner, A.: Defining a software maintainability dataset: collecting, aggregating and analysing expert evaluations of software maintainability. In: 2020 IEEE International Conference on Software Maintenance and Evolution (ICSME), pp. 278–289. IEEE (2020)

41. Schnappinger, M., Fietzke, A., Pretschner, A.: A software maintainability dataset, September 2020. https://doi.org/10.6084/m9.figshare.12801215

42. Schnappinger, M., Fietzke, A., Pretschner, A.: Human-level ordinal maintainability prediction based on static code metrics. In: Evaluation and Assessment in Software Engineering, EASE 2021, pp. 160–169 (2021)

43. Schnappinger, M., Osman, M.H., Pretschner, A., Fietzke, A.: Learning a classifier for prediction of maintainability based on static analysis tools. In: Proceedings of the 27th International Conference on Program Comprehension, pp. 243–248. IEEE (2019)

44. Schnappinger, M., Osman, M.H., Pretschner, A., Pizka, M., Fietzke, A.: Software quality assessment in practice: a hypothesis-driven framework. In: Proceedings of the 12th ACM/IEEE International Symposium on Empirical Software Engineering and Measurement, p. 40. ACM (2018)

45. Sun, C., Qiu, X., Xu, Y., Huang, X.: How to fine-tune BERT for text classification? In: Sun, M., Huang, X., Ji, H., Liu, Z., Liu, Y. (eds.) CCL 2019. LNCS (LNAI), vol. 11856, pp. 194–206. Springer, Cham (2019). https://doi.org/10.1007/978-3-030-32381-3_16

46. Van Koten, C., Gray, A.: An application of Bayesian network for predicting object-oriented software maintainability. Inf. Softw. Technol. **48**(1), 59–67 (2006)

47. Von Mayrhauser, A., Vans, A.M.: Program comprehension during software maintenance and evolution. Computer **28**(8), 44–55 (1995)

48. Wong, W.E., Gao, R., Li, Y., Abreu, R., Wotawa, F.: A survey on software fault localization. IEEE Trans. Software Eng. **42**(8), 707–740 (2016)
49. Xing, F., Guo, P., Lyu, M.R.: A novel method for early software quality prediction based on support vector machine. In: 16th IEEE International Symposium on Software Reliability Engineering (ISSRE 2005), pp. 10-pp. IEEE (2005)
50. Yao, J., Shepperd, M.: Assessing software defection prediction performance: why using the matthews correlation coefficient matters. In: Proceedings of the Evaluation and Assessment in Software Engineering, pp. 120–129 (2020)
51. Zhou, Y., Leung, H.: Predicting object-oriented software maintainability using multivariate adaptive regression splines. J. Syst. Softw. **80**(8), 1349–1361 (2007)

Quality Assurance
for Software-Intensive Systems

Specification of Passive Test Cases Using an Improved T-EARS Language

Daniel Flemström[✉][ID], Wasif Afzal[ID], and Eduard Paul Enoiu[ID]

Mälardalen University, Västerås, Sweden
{daniel.flemstrom,wasif.afzal,eduard.paul.enoiu}@mdh.se

Abstract. Test cases that only observe the system under test can improve parallelism and detection of faults occurring due to unanticipated feature interactions. Traditionally, such *passive* test cases have been challenging to express, partly due to the use of complex mathematical notations. The T-EARS (Timed Easy Approach to Requirements Syntax) language prototype was introduced to respond to this and has received positive feedback from practitioners. However, the prototype suffered from few deficiencies, such as allowing non-intuitive combinations of expressions and usage of temporal specifiers that quickly got difficult to understand. This paper builds on the T-EARS prototype and input from experienced testers on a previous iteration of the language. The collected experience was applied to a new prototype using a structured update process, including a set of system-level requirements from a vehicular software system. The results include a new, improved grammar for the T-EARS language and a description of the evaluation semantics.

1 Introduction

We trust vehicular software to be functional, safe and reliable on a daily basis. Traditionally, a great number of software tests ensure that the software works as specified. Intuitively, the more the tests can be run in parallel, the shorter each testing cycle can be and more thorough the testing. One approach that has shown promising results in dealing with this problem is passive testing using guarded assertions (G/As) [12,22]. As in contemporary passive testing or monitoring, the idea is to treat the input stimuli (that affects the system state) and the test oracle (that decides if a system requirement is fulfilled or not) independently. Consequently, if all necessary signals have been logged, passive testing allows parallel evaluation and even off-line evaluation of G/As.

A weakness with most passive testing or monitoring approaches [3] is that they rely on formal descriptions of test cases that tend to meet quite some resistance from practitioners [2,5,7] for being too complex. Although there exist predefined patterns and even graphical representations [2,7] to facilitate the formalization of either requirements or test cases, the problem of readability and traceability remains. As a reaction to such difficulties, T-EARS (Timed Easy Approach to Requirements Syntax) was proposed as an engineer-friendly

© Springer Nature Switzerland AG 2022
D. Mendez et al. (Eds.): SWQD 2022, LNBIP 439, pp. 63–83, 2022.
https://doi.org/10.1007/978-3-031-04115-0_5

approach to writing passive test cases [8]. The T-EARS language allows writing easy-to-write and easy-to-read (executable) requirements and test cases for signal-based systems such as vehicular systems. The initial versions of the approach and the language were appreciated by the test engineers [9], but still suffered from having an experimental (very open) grammar and automatic conversions that did not always evaluate as the tester expected. Unexpected evaluation results were especially common for the timing-related keywords.

The work in this paper aims to improve the T-EARS language, prototyped in [8] and [4], so the language becomes more intuitive from a testing perspective. Primarily, these refinements concern the grammar and semantics of the language. Other refinements include suggesting a set of boiler plates to decrease the distance between the EARS patterns and the final corresponding passive test cases. Finally, the intuition and usage of the temporal specification is addressed.

The results of these refinements have been implemented and evaluated in [11]. The industrial validation part of that paper analyzed 116 safety-related requirements from an ongoing industrial project at Alstom Transport AB. The refined T-EARS language and the supporting tool-chain were found to be applicable for 64% of the studied requirements. Furthermore, an expert from Alstom Transport AB performed two testing sessions to validate the applicability of the refined T-EARS language in terms of requirements coverage and fault detection respectively. The result from the first testing session showed that the translation to T-EARS was stable for a number of requirements whereas some requirements could not be evaluated due to certain signals not being logged, which is a common situation in testing at Alstom Transport AB. In the second testing session, the expert injected faults in the SUT, known to be hard to find with traditional testing. The G/As were able to detect all injected faults. In summary, the evaluation showed how passive testing with an improved language can be used to understand requirements coverage and finding faults.

Whereas [11] focus on the overall approach and evaluation, this paper focus on providing more detailed insights into the language and how we improved it. The main contributions are (i) an Ohm grammar for the improved T-EARS language and (ii) semantics descriptions for the improved T-EARS language.

2   Background

2.1   Passive Testing

Passive testing is an approach where the test cases only observes the system under test (SUT). When a testable state is detected, further observations are done to see whether the tested requirement is fulfilled or not. The concept has been used in many variants in various domains [3]. Notably, most of these works target non-vehicular software testing, such as protocol testing in web and telecom applications and are based on formal specifications.

2.2 Guarded Assertions

The concept of an independent guarded assertion (IGA) [12] or simply a guarded assertion (G/A) was introduced as an approach for system-level, passive testing of vehicular software. A G/A is defined by a *guard* expression, G, that decides whether the *assertion* expression, A, is expected to be fulfilled or not.

Let's consider the following illustrative vehicular requirement: "whenever the brake pedal is pressed, the brake light should be lit". Assuming that we successfully created a guard and an assertion expression for this example, the guard expression G would decide whether the brake pedal is pressed or not (a sequence of time intervals where the guard is true), and the assertion expression A would evaluate to true whenever the brake light is lit. For each guard interval, as long as A is true, the test is considered to be passed. Conversely, if A is false any time during the guard interval, the test had failed when A was false. Outside the guard intervals, the result of the assertion expression is not evaluated.

A previous attempt to express such G/As can be found in the SAGA (**S**ituation-based **I**ntegration **T**esting of **A**utomotive **S**ystems using **G**uarded **A**ssertions) approach [8]. The SAGA approach is the prototype of a tool chain consisting of an interactive test case editor and a description language i.e., the T-EARS language mentioned in the next section.

2.3 Easy Approach to Requirements Syntax (EARS)

The purpose of the Easy Approach to Requirements Syntax (EARS) [16] is to provide minimal syntax, helping the requirements engineer to write natural language requirements that are less ambiguous, better structured, and less complex.

While already successful for specifying requirements [14,15], we argue that by evolving the syntax to be machine-interpretable, the quality of requirements would increase, as well as the gap between requirements and testing would reduce [17,24]. The T-EARS language [4,8,10] with the accompanied SAGA-Toolkit is a first step towards such an extension of EARS.

2.4 The Ohm Grammar Language

Ohm[1] and the Arc Ohm parser library are used for specifying the grammar and semantics of a domain specific language. Such a language is defined by i) a set of terminals, ii) a grammar and iii) a set of semantic rules. Firstly, a set of terminals (such as keywords or numbers) defines what you can write, and a set of rules define how you are allowed to combine the terminals into the different constructs of the language.

While the grammar describes all acceptable strings for the described language, it does not say anything about what it means. The interpretation (or actual meaning) of the rules is called the semantics of the language.

---

[1] https://github.com/harc/ohm.

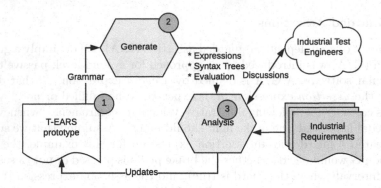

Fig. 1. Method overview

3   Method

The work of the new T-EARS version started with the prototype in [8] and a case study on the previous prototype [9] as input. The refinements were performed during a number of iterations as illustrated in Fig. 1. Each iteration started with (an updated version of) the T-EARS prototype. For the first iterations, we systematically generated possible expressions and syntax trees by hand. For each of those expressions, we (manually and independently) created a sketch of the intuitive evaluation of the expression (according to our understanding and discussions with test engineers at Scania and Alstom Transport AB). Possible and required expressions were sorted into useful expressions and expressions that should be forbidden (bad expressions). Further, to ensure the expressiveness of he language, a set of 40 safety-critical requirements from Alstom Transport AB and a complex requirement from Scania CV AB were used for the static evaluation of the language updates. The set of useful expressions was then analyzed against a set of evaluation questions concerning, e.g., usefulness, completeness and intuitiveness. Based on this analysis, the prototype grammar, the translated requirements, and the useful expressions were updated until the expressions and the grammar was consistent. This process was repeated until the requirements could be expressed as passive test cases using the updated language, leading to test cases that were easy to understand and interpret. During parallel work with industrial adoption of passive testing using the refined T-EARS language [11], a set of tuning keywords were added to ignore false fails. With all refinements in place, 116 safety critical requirements were analyzed in [11] to determine the applicability of the final results.

4   Result: The Updated T-EARS Language

T-EARS provides six boilerplates as shown in Listing 1.1. Just as EARS, T-EARS reasons about system states and system events. A system state can be represented as a binary signal that is true when the system is in the specified

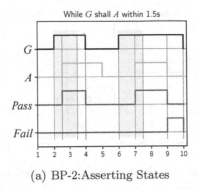

(a) BP-2:Asserting States

Fig. 2. State boilerplate example. Shadow = grace period of 1.5 s (Color figure online)

state and false when the system is considered to be in another state. State is internally represented as a series of time intervals (while state is true), and events are represented as a series of time-stamps. In the text, we use the binary signal metaphor and intervals interchangeably.

```
'Bp-1' = while true            shall <sys response state A>
'Bp-2' = while <sys state G > shall <sys response state A> within t
'Bp-3' = when <events G> shall <sys response state A> within t
'Bp-4' = when <events G> shall <response events A> within t
'Bp-5' = when <events G> shall <sys response state A> for tf within tw
'Bp-6' = when <events G> shall <sys response state A> within tw for tf
```

Listing 1.1. Resulting T-EARS Boilerplates, sys = system

The rest of this section outlines how each EARS pattern (one through six) is realized in T-EARS. The observant reader will note that, while T-EARS, in general, follows the EARS structure and usage of keywords, the syntax **the** <*system name*> is not used in T-EARS. Instead, T-EARS assumes the system name to be implicit by the signal expressions to facilitate automatic evaluation of the final passive test cases. Further, when describing the patterns, the system state and response are represented as intervals or states only. More details on how to combine signals and operators to express such states and events using logged data are covered separately in Sects. 4.8–4.11.

Ubiquitous: A ubiquitous requirement describes a property of the system that should always hold, e.g., "the big red emergency lamp should never be lit". In T-EARS this is realized by the first boiler plate. The result is a pass whenever the state assertion A is true and failed for not (A).

State-Driven: A state-driven requirement describes a property of the system that should hold as long as it is in a particular state. E.g., "**while** the vehicle is moving **shall** doors be locked". In T-EARS, BP-2 is used for such requirements. Figure 2 shows that, in general, during the specified guard intervals (G == true in Fig. 2), a pass (P == true in Fig. 2) is reported whenever the assertion is true, and a fail (F==true in Fig. 2) whenever the assertion is false. While passes are duly reported during the whole guard intervals, fails during each within-period

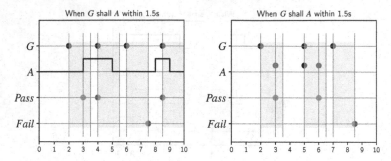

(a) BP-3: Asserting State Response(b) BP-4: Asserting Event Response

Fig. 3. Event boilerplates evaluation examples (Color figure online)

(yellow shadow in Fig. 2) are ignored. The within period starts at each guard interval and have the length specified after the `within` keyword. Outside the guard intervals, the value of the assertion is ignored.

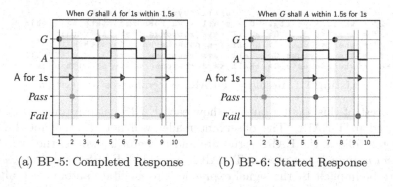

(a) BP-5: Completed Response   (b) BP-6: Started Response

Fig. 4. Boilerplate evaluation examples (Color figure online)

Event-Driven: An event driven requirement describes an expected response to a (series of) discrete event(s). E.g, "**when** horn button is pushed **shall** the horn honk". T-EARS provides a few variations for this pattern for asserting event responses or a state response. The first, **BP-3** is used for asserting a system state response within a timeout whenever an event occurs. The intuition is that for each guard event, one pass is reported as soon as the assertion is true. However, if the assertion is not true any time before the timeout t, a fail is reported at g $+ t$. Figure 3a shows how this boilerplate is evaluated for four guard events. The yellow shadow shows the within t period occurring after each guard event. For the first guard event (at 2 s) A becomes true just before the within interval ends and a pass is reported. When second guard event occurs (at 4 s), A is already true and a pass is reported immediately. For the third guard event (g_3 at 6 s), the system response A does not occur within t and a fail is reported at $g_3 + t$.

Finally, the last guard (at 8.5 s) is immediately pass since A is already true. **BP-4** is used for asserting a system event within a timeout t as shown in Fig. 3b. The semantics follows BP-3. A pass is reported if a response event (A) occurs before the within period ends, and a fail is reported at $g + t$ if no event occurred. For the first guard (2 s) an event is found before the within period (in yellow) ends. A pass is reported at that time. For the second guard event (at 5 s), there is an event a at 5 s. Since this event occurred at the same time as the guard event, it cannot be a response to that guard event and is thus ignored. Instead next event in A that occurs at 6 s yields a pass since it is still inside the within period. For the third guard event (at 7 s) no response in A occurs and as for BP-3, a fail is reported at $g + t$ (8.5 s). There are also two boiler plates for asserting a system state of a particular length. The first, **BP-5**, requires the system state to be tf long and finish within tw. Figure 4a shows three examples on how this boilerplate is evaluated. For the first guard event, A is already true. The for 1s period is counted from guard and results in an event if A stays true for 1.5 s. This event is evaluated as in BP-3. For the next guard, A becomes true at 5 s, so we start counting the 1.5 s from here. However, the within period ends before the 1.5 s could be completed. A fail is thus reported at $g + t$ as for BP-3. For the last guard event, A is not true long enough, but since the within period ends first, this does not matter and a fail is reported at $g + t$. BP-6 is used for asserting that a response state of (min) length tg is initiated within tw from each guard event. Figure 4b illustrates the difference between BP-6 and BP-5. With G and A the same, we note that for the second guard event, we allow the for period (the arrows in the figure) to stretch outside the within period (yellow shadow in the figure). As a consequence, the second guard events results in a pass when A has been true for 1.5 s after the guard event. For the last guard event, we still get a fail, but the fail is reported because the for period could not be fulfilled (slightly later than the BP-5 example).

Option: Some requirements are only applicable to certain configurations of the SUT. E.g., "**where** the vehicle has a horn, [*horn requirement*]". In T-EARS this is accomplished by using the where <*boolean expression*> before a G/A boilerplate. In contrast to a guard expression (that varies over the time covered in the log-file), this is a single Boolean value that concerns the whole log-file.

Unwanted Behavior: Some behaviors are unwanted but still require a response. E.g., "**if** oil pressure is critical **then** the motor should shut down". In T-EARS, there is no **if**, or **then**-keyword, however unwanted behavior can modeled by using the existing boilerplates.

Complex: More complex requirements can be constructed by *combining* the EARS patterns. E.g **when** the honk button is pressed **while** engine is running shall horn honk. In the new version of T-EARS, nesting while and when expressions were removed in favor to stricter rules on how to combine states and events to form guard expressions. Instead of nesting the when and while expression, above expression is expressed using the more structured rules of Events and Intervals, as *when honk button is pressed and engine is running shall horn honk*.

In the upcoming sections, we present the grammar developed to realize these boilerplates.

4.1 Keyword Terminals

The terminals grammar block defines a rule for each keyword and also groups the keywords into a logical group:

```
1    keyword =
2    /  1.          2.        3.          4.        5.          */
3      where   | and | for     | true   | const
4      | when  | or  | within  | false  | alias
5      | while       | longer  | inf    | def
6      | shall       | shorter         | events
7                    | than            | intervals
8                    | at
9    /*6*/
10   |allow|fail|ignore
```

Listing 1.2. Non-trivial Terminals

The first group of keywords outlines the G/A (e.g., `where`, `when`). The conjunctions group (`and`, `or`) allows composing expressions. The third group consists of the timing modifiers (`for`, `within` etc.). The fourth group has a set of built-in constants (`true`, `false`, `inf`). The fifth group concerns structuring the expressions (e.g., `def`, `alias`, `const`).

4.2 Structural Elements

The structural elements block defines the following main rules:

```
1    Constant =
2        const identifier "=" (Timeout | Num | Boolean)
3    IntervalsDef =
4        def intervals identifier "=" Intervals
5
6    EventsDef   =
7        def events    identifier "=" Events
8
9    Alias = alias identifier "=" identifier
```

Listing 1.3. Structural Elements

The purpose of the rule *Constant* in Listing 1.3 is to define named constants, e.g., limits or timeouts. The constant is checked by the corresponding semantic operation of the rule where the constant is used. A constant can only be defined once within a test case context. The purpose of the rules *IntervalsDef* and *EventsDef* is to structure sub-expressions into named expressions to increase readability. A def expression can only be defined once using the same name. Further, the keywords `events, intervals` facilitates type checking while typing the expressions in the interactive editor. The expression is evaluated where used (not where it is defined). The `alias` keyword renames an identifier. An alias can be redefined, allowing the same alias in two G/As to have different meanings.

Since an alias is resolved where it is evaluated, using an alias inside a named expression offers a primitive way of user-defined functions. Another purpose of the alias keyword is to create abstractions for, e.g., release or variant of a system without changing the test logic.

4.3   Basic Data Types

There are four basic types, Boolean, Float, Integer, and Time. Listing 1.4 shows how they are defined. The example shows the Boolean type. One sub rule defines explicit usage (e.g., true, false) and one rule allows using an identifier (e.g., $--constOrAlias$). The identifier rule allows using a constant or alias (an alias is a renamed constant). There is also a main rule for how identifiers can be specified. The *identifier–quoted* allows strings in quotes that would otherwise be forbidden.

```
1   Boolean = (true | false)              --bool
2           | identifier                  --constOrAlias
3
4   identifier ="'" idstring_quoted  "'"  --quoted
5           | idstring
6   //--------------------------------------------------
7   idstring = ~digit ~keyword letter+ (specialChar | alnum)*
8   idstring_quoted = (specialChar | mustQuoteChar | alnum)+
9   specialChar   = ( "_" | "/" | "[" | "]" | "." | "/" | ":")
10  mustQuoteChar = "-" | "+" | " " | "(" | ")"
11
12  sign = ("+" | "-")
13  TimeUnit = ("s"~"h | "ms"~"h")
```
Listing 1.4. Basic Data types

Examples of such strings are strings that contain spaces or keywords. The support rules below row 7 in Listing 1.4 shows the details of, e.g., sign and string handling. The tilde operator followed by the letter h (at line 13 in the listing) prevents the time unit to be confused with the keyword shall.

4.4   Signals Data Type

In a signal based system, the input and output consists of a set of (single value) signals that vary over time. Example signals are actuator readings, signals from other subsystems, and even sampled continuous values such as speed or temperature. These signals can be recorded into log files and fetched by name when building T-EARS expressions. Using the T-EARS editor [8, 11], it is also possible to manually construct *abstract* signals to allow executable examples for higher-level requirements. In T-EARS, there are also several ways to manipulate signals as described by the *Signals* grammar block:

```
1   Signal =
2         Signal SigOP Signal        --sigOpSig
3       | SignalFunction             --func
4       | (true | false | NUM)       --constant
5       | identifier                 --sigAliasConst
6       | "(" Signal ")"             --parentheses
7
```

```
8    SigOp =
9      ( "+" | "-" | "/" | "*")
10
11   SignalFunction =
12      derivative "(" (Timeout ",")? Signal ")"
13      | abs "(" Signal ")"
14      | bitmask "(" IntegerOrConst "," Signal ")"
15      | count "(" Events "," Intervals ")"
16      | maxVal "(" NonemptyListOf< Signal, ","> ")"
17      | select "(" Signal "," Signal "," Signal ")"
18      | exists "(" identifier ")"
```

Listing 1.5. The Signal Datatype

The rules Listing 1.5 defines the Signal data type. Besides the main rule *Signal*, there are two support rules: *SigOp* defines trivial mathematical operations on two signals, and, *SignalFunction*, that defines all built-in functions that return a value of type Signal.

In more detail, the Signal data type is represented by a series of samples [time, value] pairs and is denoted with the letter S (Signal). In the examples below, we use the notation $S = [s_0, \ldots, s_m]$ for a signal with $m + 1$ samples, where each sample ([time, value] pair) is noted as $s_i = [t_i, v_i]$. Logs may be sampled with a variable sampling rate, so the value between one sample is considered to be constant until the next sample.

When evaluating mathematical expressions (line 2, $--sigOpSig$), the signals are projected on a common timeline. The operator (e.g., plus or minus) is then applied on each sample along the common timeline. The $--func$ sub-rule at line 3 allows more advanced signal processing in the functions listed by the support rule *SignalFunctions*. The currently provided functions are **derivative**, a forward approximating derivative with an optional threshold to smooth out the result over several samples as $s_n(i) = \frac{v_{n+i} - v_n}{t_{n+i} - t_n}$. The threshold t makes sure to increase i from 1 until $i : t < t_{n+i} - t_n$. Increasing the threshold widens the delta in the approximation. The **abs** function processes each sample of a signal as $v_n = abs(v_n)$. The **bitmask** function returns $v_n = v_n \wedge bitmask$, applied on each sample of a signal. The **count** function takes two arguments: one Events and one Intervals argument. The result is a signal with the number of events during the interval of r_i as value. The value is constant during each interval of r_i. The **maxVal** function takes a list of Signals and returns a new Signal with the largest sample value at each sampled point in time. The **select** function selects samples from the second or third signal argument depending on the first signal argument's value. Where the first signal argument equals true, the sample from the second signal is used. Otherwise, the sample from the third signal argument is used. If the first expression is constant, only the used signal needs to be defined. The **exists** function returns a signal that is constant true if there exists a signal with the name of the given identifier. Typically, the last two functions, **select** and **exists**, are often used together to enable default values for optional signals.

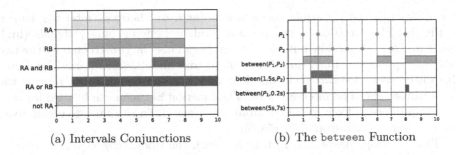

(a) Intervals Conjunctions   (b) The between Function

Fig. 5. Interval operations and creation. R denotes intervals, P denotes events

The sub-rule at line four in the listing ($--constant$) defines a pseudo-signal with a constant value. The signal is defined over the logged min and max time. It is possible to specify a binary or a numerical value.

If an identifier is specified ($--sigAliasConst$, sub-rule at line five), this may refer to a signal name to fetch from a loaded log file, an alias, or a named constant. If the identifier is an alias, the alias is resolved until a signal name or a constant is found. A constant (sub rule $--constant$) is interpreted as a signal with a constant value over the entire log file.

4.5   Intervals Data Type

The syntactical rules for Intervals are presented in Listing 1.6.

```
1   Intervals =
2       IntervalsExpr  TimeFilter*
3       ((and|or)
4       IntervalsExpr  TimeFilter*  )*    --conj
5
6   TimeFilter  =
7       longer than  Timeout              --atLeast
8     | shorter than  Timeout             --atMost
9
10  IntervalsExpr (Interval Expression) =
11    | "(" Intervals ")"                 --parentheses
12    | IntervalFunction                  --func
13    | Signal RelOp Signal               --relop
14    | (true | false)                    --boolean
15    | definedIntervals                  --definition
16    | "[" ListOf<Interval, ","> "]" --list
17
18  Interval = "[" Timeout "," Timeout "]"
19
20  RelOp =    ("==" | "!=" | "~=" | ">=" | ">" | "<=" | "<")
21
22  IntervalFunction =
23        not "(" Intervals ")"
24      | between "(" (Events|Timeout) ","
25                    (Events|Timeout) ")"
```

Listing 1.6. The Intervals Datatype

The first rule at lines 1–4 in Listing 1.6, together with the support rule (*TimeFilter* at lines 6–9), allows filtering intervals shorter or longer than a specified threshold. The filters can be defined in any order. The rule at lines 1–4 also defines the two possible conjunctions (**and, or**) between intervals, shown in Fig. 5a. The intuition is the same as and/or between binary signals (high inside an interval and low outside). Intervals can also be constructed by the two built-in support functions (line 12: $--func$, and lines 22–25: *IntervalFunction*). Currently, there are two such functions defined. The function **not** returns the two-complement of an interval series. The function **between** can be used for constructing intervals from Events or from one event and a constant, to create fixed length events, as illustrated in Fig. 5b.

The $--relop$ rule at line 13 together with the rule *RelOp* at line 20 defines how signals and relational operators are combined to form Intervals. The signals are projected onto a common timeline (each unique sample time from both signals) and each sample is compared using the operator. Again, it should be noted that values are not interpolated between samples. The rule at line 16 ($--list$) and line 18 (*Interval*) defines manual specification of an intervals series. The time can be specified numerically, but also by using named constants.

4.6   Events Data Type

The Events data type describes how to compose a series of system events. The rules for the Events data type are presented in Listing 1.7 and Fig. 6.

```
1   Events =
2       Intervals ForExpression      --intervalFor
3       | Events    and Intervals    --andIntervals
4       | Intervals and Events       --intervalAnd
5       | Events or  Events          --eventsOr
6       | Events ("+"|"-") Timeout    --nudge
7       | EventFunctions             --function
8       | definedEvents              --definition
9       | "[" ListOf<Timeout, ","> "]"  --list
10      | "(" Events ")"             --parenthesis
11
12  EventFunction =
13      risingEdge  "(" Intervals ")"
14      | fallingEdge "(" Intervals ")"
15      | cycle "(" (Events ",")? Timeout ")"
```

Listing 1.7. The Events Datatype

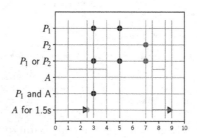

Fig. 6. Evaluation examples of the event rules

The first rule at line 2 in Listing 1.7 ($--intervalFor$) defines events as a response to a timeout on an interval. The result is one event for each interval, long enough to reach the timeout as $P = [r_s+t]\forall r : r_s+t < r_e$, where R is a series of intervals with each interval starting at r_s and ending at r_e. The next two rules at lines 3–4 ($--andIntervals$, $--intervalAnd$) defines the **and** operator between Intervals and Events. The intuition is that the events occurring during an interval are kept. Note that the rule P_1 *and* $P2$ is removed from the language. The reason is that events are represented by high resolution timestamps and would need to be identical to yield any results, which is not realistic. A workaround is to replace P with acceptable intervals around each event in P, as in the following example:

$$W = between(P - t, P + t) \tag{1}$$

$$P \textbf{ and } Q \Rightarrow Q \textbf{ and } W \tag{2}$$

The interval W represents an interval that is reasonably close to P. The points in Q that reside in any of these intervals will be kept. It should be noted that if the interval is constructed using the points of Q instead, the result would be the points in P that match an interval. Also, the time t needs to be sufficiently small to not create overlapping intervals in W.

Line 5 in Listing 1.7 ($--eventsOr$) shows the only conjunction between Events. The expression P_1 *or* P_2 would evaluate to all events in P_1 and P_2, sorted and with duplicates removed.

Line 6 ($--nudge$) shows how each event can be pushed forward or backward in time. The expression $P_1 + t$ would evaluate in a series events $[p + t] \ \forall p \in P_1$.

For more complex Events operations, there are some built-in functions that takes other data types as input and returns Events (Line 8 ($--function$) and lines 12–15 ($EventFunction$)). Currently, there are three such functions defined. The first two concerns edge detection. Detecting the edges of signals or intervals is common in creating events based on signal or interval features. Since intervals are conceptually treated as a binary signal, rising edge and falling edge correspond to each interval's start and end. The last function is requested by test engineers to ensure that cyclic events are correctly sent on the CAN bus. The first argument is an optional event series. The cycle will start at the first event in this series and continue as long as the last logged sample (in the currently loaded log). The second argument defines the cycle width.

The rule $--list$ on line 9 in Listing 1.7, allows to hand-craft en Event series by assigning *individual* time points to an Events. These time points may be either specified as (milli) seconds or by using a constant or alias for a constant.

Finally, the $--definition$ rule allows for using a defined events-expression. When evaluated, any level of aliases are resolved and eventually, the defined Events expression is evaluated.

4.7 Boolean Expressions

The EARS pattern **Option** is realized by the **where** keyword and a Boolean expression. This Boolean expression decides if the G/A should be evaluated at all or not. The grammar for Boolean is shown in Listing 1.8.

```
1    BoolExpr = BoolExpr (and|or) BoolExpr          --conj
2         | BoolExpr ("==" | "!=") BoolExpr         --eq
3         | Num RelationalOperator Num              --op
4         | BooleanFunction                         --func
5         | Boolean                                 --boolean
6         | identifier                              --constOrAlias
7         | "(" BoolExpr ")"                        --para
8
9    Boolean = (true | false )
10   BooleanFunction =
11        exists "(" identifier ")"                 --exists
```

Listing 1.8. The BoolExpr Datatype

4.8 Guarded Assertion Rules

There are two types of guarded assertions: The State G/A, observes the system state and expects some requirements to be held during this time. These are specified using the `while` keyword as shown in line 4 in Listing 1.9. The second type is the Event G/A that reacts to events and checks a requirement in response to the events. Event G/As are specified using the `When` keyword as shown in line 5 in Listing 1.9. Both rules are build up by a guard rule and an optional assertion rule.

```
1    GA = ((identifier "=")? Config? GuardedAssertion)
2    Config = where BoolExpr
3    GuardedAssertion =
4        while Intervals (shall IntervalAssertion)?
5      | when   Events   (shall EventsAssertion)?
6
7    IntervalAssertion = Intervals (within Timeout)?
8
9    EventsAssertion =
10        Intervals for Timeout within Timeout
11      | Events within Timeout
12      | Intervals (within Timeout)? (for Timeout)?
```

Listing 1.9. Guarded Assertions

The Events assertion is a bit more complicated with three rules. The first rule at line 10 in Listing 1.9 shows the case when the response to an event is that the system enters the state (described by Intervals) for a time (first Timeout expression). If the system is kept in the asserted state for that time, a pass is emitted for the guard at that time $(g + t)$. If the system does not enter the asserted state, a fail is emitted as soon as the asserted state does not hold. The above must have been completed before the within period of the guard ends.

The second Event Assertion rule in line 11 in Listing 1.9 shows the case when an assertion event is expected as a response to a guard event. If an assertion event can be detected before the within period of a guard ends, a pass is emitted for that guard at that time. If no event is detected, a fail is emitted at the end of the within period. If the guard events are very close in time, the same assertion event can satisfy several guards.

The third rule in line 12 in Listing 1.9 shows the case when a state of a particular length is required to start within the specified time. The difference to the rule in line 10 is that the assertion for-period does not need to be finished before the within period of the guard ends. If the system is already in the asserted state, time is counted from the start of the guard.

4.9   Miscellaneous Modifiers

The statement `ignore` $<|>$ *timeout* tells the evaluation core to ignore any fails before or after the specified time. This is used when there are disturbances at startup or shut down of the system under test. There is also a statement `Allow` *timout* `fail` that makes the G/A ignores fails of the specified length. It is typically used to rule our sampling errors that may lead to fails due to the assertion appears to change before the guard due to sampling errors.

4.10   Timing Considerations

Another core feature of T-EARS, partially present in the early prototypes, is the possibility to specify timing information in logical expressions. Using the keyword `for`, the length of an interval could be specified and using the keyword `within`, timeouts, or grace times could be specified. Further research, however, revealed that longer expressions with the timing keywords applied to each sub-expression were difficult to comprehend or even evaluate correctly. One culprit was that the `for` keyword filtered out intervals longer than the specified timeout, regardless of the expression context, which sometimes yielded very confusing results. The reason is that we, as human readers, have different expectations on what effect `for` has, depending on the expression context. Our solution is to separate different filtering expectations into different keywords. The construction `longer than` and `shorter than` as described in Sect. 4.5 filters intervals with respect to length, regardless of the current context. Concerning the `for` keyword, the new grammar considers the perception of relative time base: Consider the expressions R `for` 10 s. Regarding R as a binary signal, the expression evaluates to one event each time the signal has been true for 10 s. At first glance, this seems to be an exact definition, but putting the expression into different contexts reveals some interesting properties.

In the context of a guard expression, we expect (R for 4 s) to be "measured" from the start of each interval in R, resulting in a series of events, say $[p_1, p_2, \ldots, p_n]$. In the assertion context, however, there is an implicit assumption that the assertion evaluation is a consequence of a guard event (or interval) and hence, (R for 4 s) is expected to be measured from each p_i in the guard expression, i.e., the time for the associated guard. As a consequence of the potential for confusion, the new T-EARS restricts the usage and the meaning of the `for` keyword, as described in Sect. 4.5 and 4.8. Mixing the `for` keyword with the `within` keyword makes things even more complicated. Further, the effect of `within..for` is different from the effect of `for..within` on an expression.

4.11   General Structure of a T-EARS Test Case

Putting the pieces together, Listing 1.10 illustrates a minor test case:

```
1    //-------------- REQ 558-S1-------------
2    // While the vehicle is underway with a speed more thatn 10 km/h,
3    // the doors shall be locked.
4
5    //////// Abstract G/A   /////////
6    //def intervals MOVING      = [[5s,30s],[100s,300s]]
7    //def intervals DOOR_LOCKED = [[6s,31s],[120s,300s]] // PASS,FAIL
8
9    //// G/A Concretization (Can be centralized in a main def file) /////
10   // System version 1.2.4
11   const DOORS = 1
12   const DOOR_LOCKED_MASK  = 8
13
14   def intervals MOVING =
15       MWT_Standstill == false and MWT_BUS2_Speed > 10
16   def intervals DOOR_LOCKED =
17       bitmask(DOOR_LOCKED_MASK,MWT_door_lock) == DOOR_LOCKED_MASK
18
19   // G/A Definition(s)
20   '558-S1' = where DOORS > 0
21             while MOVING == true
22             shall DOOR_LOCKED == true within 3s
```

Listing 1.10. General Structure of a T-EARS Script

In the example (Listing 1.10), there are three regions of particular interest. The first region (Line 1–7) contains requirement information and example data for an abstract G/A, followed by a region with structural elements (lines 10–17) that make G/As easier to read. These connect the abstract signals to expressions of actual log data. If aliases, constants, and definitions are common to many G/As, they are typically put in a shared file instead. The last region of interest at lines 19–22 is where the actual passive test case is defined. Any number of named G/As can be specified.

5 Discussion on T-EARS Improvement

The early prototypes of the T-EARS language allowed experimenting with a great variety of expressions that could be defined and evaluated against real industrial requirements. Many of these were useful, while others turned out to be less useful. In this work, the goal is to promote useful expressions while suppressing less useful ones and updating the language to be more complete and intuitive. Thus, the goal here concerns updates of the language constructs to improve readability without losing expressiveness. We achieved this goal through a minimal set of top-level boilerplates, introducing strong typing, restricting the usage of timing keywords, and defining new keywords to avoid ambiguous definitions. Although the sum of keywords and language constructs added outgrew the ones removed, the result is a language that more clearly corresponds to the EARS patterns. Instead of automatic conversions between events and intervals, there are now only a few well-defined ways of constructing expressions between the types. One operation that was explicitly removed was (*Event* **and**

Event). Since this would require the timestamps to be precisely matching, allowing such an operation would, in practice, only add confusion to the test cases. When the new restricted grammar was applied to old T-EARS expressions, it revealed quite a few misunderstandings regarding events/intervals. Concerning the expressiveness, the first three EARS patterns (Ubiquitous, State-Drive, and, Event-Driven) are (still) wholly covered by the G/A boilerplates. The fourth EARS pattern (Option) was a strong suggestion from the testers in the case study [9]. The testers wished to have conditionally evaluated G/As depending on configuration information and other G/As. Here rudimentary support was added for Boolean expressions and constants. However, it is still not possible to use the activation or result of a G/A to turn on/off others' evaluations. The fifth EARS pattern can be accomplished but the keywords **if** and **then** may introduce confusion around states or events and are thus not included in T-EARS. The sixth EARS pattern (complex) allows mixing while and when which generated expressions that were inherently difficult to understand. The complex EARS pattern is instead realized in T-EARS using the well defined composition rules of Events and Intervals. Another vital requirement from the testers was user-defined functions. Albeit rather crude, this is now possible in T-EARS since the definitions are evaluated late, and aliases can be used as parameters for the definitions.

Finally, a word about timing. While the early T-EARS prototypes used the **for**-keyword as a filter (keeping all intervals longer than the specified timeout), the tester's expectations differed depending on where the keyword was specified. In some cases, an event was expected after the timeout. In other cases, intervals of precisely the length of the timeout. Further, when the **for** expression was used in an assertion, their semantic meaning was unclear. The remedy was to remove the filtering semantics altogether and introduce keywords for filtering (**longer than, shorter than**), while the **for** keyword was restricted to a few consistent meanings. Further, moving the **within** keyword from individual sub-expressions to the G/A boilerplate reduced confusion. Consider the example: R_1 *for* 10 s *and* P_1 *within* 2 s *or* P_2 *within* 4 s. In the example, it is not clear where the time starts. Using the left-hand side of the sequence operator, or the guard as the time base for the timing specifications **within** the evaluation of the timeouts became consistent with the expectations of the testers' intuition.

6 Related Work

This work relates to passive testing, specification of test cases, and the tool support for the use of passive testing and specification of such test cases. We rely on the work of independent guarded assertions [12,22] introduced for increasing the testing parallelism in the vehicular domain. An earlier approach to guarded assertions has been evaluated by Rodriguez Navas et al. [22] and a model-checker has been used for both modelling and test case execution. In this paper, we improve upon this by translating these test cases directly from requirements. Regarding the testability of such requirements, Pudlitz et al. [19,20] used a markup language by relying on annotations of the natural language. Different from this approach, our improved T-EARS language is using a temporal specification of requirements. All these approaches are similar to the passive testing technique as it is outlined by Cavalli et al. [3] and also relate to run-time verification [13,23]. Since the use of these techniques relies on the formal specification of test cases, several researchers have attempted to use patterns and graphical models for the formalization of both requirements and test cases [1,2,7,25]. The specification of passive testing using the improved T-EARS takes another route by focusing on simplicity and closeness to the requirements text. T-EARS is based on an Easy Approach to Requirements Syntax (EARS), proposed by Rolls-Royce for the creation of semi-structured natural language requirements [16]. EARS has been used in several domains and has been shown to be useful for handling real-world requirements [14,15]. Regarding the tooling for the specification of passive test cases, several researchers have focused on providing support for specification patterns [6,18] and creating monitors and guarded assertions in Matlab [26]. Related to runtime monitoring, Rabiser et al. [21] developed a domain-specific language for defining and checking constraints at runtime.

7   Conclusion and Future Work

We have presented an updated T-EARS language grammar together with a semi-formal specification of the semantics behind the language. The update consists of a careful re-definition of the grammar and semantics for e.g., test case structure and temporal specification. By restricting the possible G/A patterns to a few well-defined boilerplates, the language and its new evaluation core now have a closer correspondence to the EARS patterns. These boilerplates also match the intuition of the testers better. The intuition is also increased by making the notation of timeouts context-dependent, i.e., the guard time domain is now a natural base for the assertion time domain.

Although T-EARS has taken a significant step forward, there are still some features deferred to future research. The first one primarily concerns the accompanied evaluation-core of the T-EARS language. While not necessary from an evaluation point of view, other attempts to create more user-friendly specification languages provide semantic mappings to proven temporal logic such as MITL or LTL. Creating such a mapping for T-EARS would allow certified evaluation tools rather than JavaScript that is used today. Such a mapping would also move the T-EARS evaluation from the offline to the online domain. Another issue is that, while the grammar supports specifying negative time like **when P_G shall P_A within** $- t$, the current semantics do not. Finally, specifying an evaluation aggregation policy for passive testing is needed to allow a drill-down analysis approach on the increased number of results.

Acknowledgement. The work in this study has received funding from the European Union's Horizon 2020 research and innovation program under grant agreement Nos.

871319, 957212; from the Swedish Innovation Agency (Vinnova) through the XIVT project and from the ECSEL Joint Undertaking (JU) under grant agreement No. 101007350.

References

1. Asteasuain, F., Braberman, V.: Specification patterns can be formal and still easy. In: International Conference on Software Engineering and Knowledge Engineering (SEKE 2001), pp. 430–436. Knowledge Systems Institute is a Graduate School, Knowledge Systems Institute (2010)
2. Autili, M., Grunske, L., Lumpe, M., Pelliccione, P., Tang, A.: Aligning qualitative, real-time, and probabilistic property specification patterns using a structured English grammar. IEEE Trans. Softw. Eng. 41(7), 620–638 (2015)
3. Cavalli, A.R., Higashino, T., Núñez, M.: A survey on formal active and passive testing with applications to the cloud. Ann. Telecommun. 70(3), 85–93 (2015). https://doi.org/10.1007/s12243-015-0457-8
4. Daniel, F., Eduard, E., Wasif, A., Daniel, S., Thomas, G., Avenir, K.: From natural language requirements to passive test cases using guarded assertions. In: International Conference on Software Quality, Reliability and Security (QRS 2018), pp. 470–481. IEEE Computer Society (2018)
5. Dwyer, M.B., Avrunin, G.S., Corbett, J.C.: Patterns in property specifications for finite-state verification. In: International Conference on Software Engineering (ICSE 1999), pp. 411–420. Association for Computing Machinery (1999). https://doi.org/10.1145/302405.302672
6. Filipovikj, P., Jagerfield, T., Nyberg, M., Rodriguez-Navas, G., Seceleanu, C.: Integrating pattern-based formal requirements specification in an industrial tool-chain. In: International Computer Software and Applications Conference (COMPSAC 2016), vol. 2, pp. 167–173. IEEE Computer Society (2016)
7. Filipovikj, P., Nyberg, M., Rodriguez-Navas, G.: Reassessing the pattern-based approach for formalizing requirements in the automotive domain. In: International Requirements Engineering Conference (RE 2014), Los Alamitos, CA, USA, pp. 444–450. IEEE Computer Society, August 2014. https://doi.org/10.1109/RE.2014. 6912296
8. Flemström, D., Gustafsson, T., Kobetski, A.: Saga toolbox: interactive testing of guarded assertions. In: International Conference on Software Testing, Verification and Validation (ICST 2017), pp. 516–523. IEEE Computer Society (2017)
9. Flemström, D., Gustafsson, T., Kobetski, A.: A case study of interactive development of passive tests. In: International Workshop on Requirements Engineering and Testing (RET 2018), pp. 13–20. Association for Computing Machinery, New York (2018). https://doi.org/10.1145/3195538.3195544
10. Flemström, D., Gustafsson, T., Kobetski, A., Sundmark, D.: A research roadmap for test design in automated integration testing of vehicular systems. In: International Conference on Fundamentals and Advances in Software Systems Integration (FASSI 2016) (2016)
11. Flemström, D., Jonsson, H., Enoiu, E.P., Afzal, W.: Industrial scale passive testing with T-EARS. In: Conference on Software Testing, Verification and Validation (ICST 2021), Los Alamitos, CA, USA, pp. 351–361. IEEE Computer Society, April 2021. https://doi.org/10.1109/ICST49551.2021.00047

12. Gustafsson, T., Skoglund, M., Kobetski, A., Sundmark, D.: Automotive system testing by independent guarded assertions. In: International Conference on Software Testing, Verification and Validation Workshops (ICSTW 2015), pp. 1–7. IEEE Computer Society (2015). https://doi.org/10.1109/ICSTW.2015.7107474

13. Leucker, M., Schallhart, C.: A brief account of runtime verification. J. Log. Algebraic Program. **78**(5), 293–303 (2009)

14. Mavin, A., Wilkinson, P.: Big ears (the return of "easy approach to requirements engineering"). In: International Conference on Requirements Engineering (RE 2010), Los Alamitos, CA, USA, pp. 277–282. IEEE Computer Society, October 2010. https://doi.org/10.1109/RE.2010.39

15. Mavin, A., Wilksinson, P., Gregory, S., Uusitalo, E.: Listens learned (8 lessons learned applying EARS). In: International Requirements Engineering Conference (RE 2016), Los Alamitos, CA, USA, pp. 276–282. IEEE Computer Society, September 2016. https://doi.org/10.1109/RE.2016.38

16. Mavin, A., Wilkinson, P., Harwood, A., Novak, M.: Easy approach to requirements syntax (EARS). In: International Requirements Engineering Conference (RE 2009), pp. 317–322. IEEE Computer Society (2009)

17. Merz, F., Sinz, C., Post, H., Gorges, T., Kropf, T.: Bridging the gap between test cases and requirements by abstract testing. Innov. Syst. Softw. Eng. **11**, 233–242 (2015). https://doi.org/10.1007/s11334-015-0245-7

18. Miao, W., Wang, X., Liu, S.: A tool for supporting requirements formalization based on specification pattern knowledge. In: International Symposium on Theoretical Aspects of Software Engineering (TASE 2015). IEEE Computer Society (2015). https://doi.org/10.1109/TASE.2015.13

19. Pudlitz, F., Brokhausen, F., Vogelsang, A.: What am i testing and where? Comparing testing procedures based on lightweight requirements annotations. Empir. Softw. Eng. **25**(4), 2809–2843 (2020). https://doi.org/10.1007/s10664-020-09815-w

20. Pudlitz, F., Vogelsang, A., Brokhausen, F.: A lightweight multilevel markup language for connecting software requirements and simulations. In: Knauss, E., Goedicke, M. (eds.) REFSQ 2019. LNCS, vol. 11412, pp. 151–166. Springer, Cham (2019). https://doi.org/10.1007/978-3-030-15538-4_11

21. Rabiser, R., Thanhofer-Pilisch, J., Vierhauser, M., Grünbacher, P., Egyed, A.: Developing and evolving a DSL-based approach for runtime monitoring of systems of systems. Autom. Softw. Eng. **25**(4), 875–915 (2018). https://doi.org/10.1007/s10515-018-0241-x

22. Rodriguez-Navas, G., Kobetski, A., Sundmark, D., Gustafsson, T.: Offline analysis of independent guarded assertions in automotive integration testing. In: International Conference on Embedded Software and Systems (ICESS 2015), pp. 1066–1073. IEEE Computer Society (2015). https://doi.org/10.1109/HPCC-CSS-ICESS.2015.251

23. Selyunin, K., Nguyen, T., Bartocci, E., Grosu, R.: Applying runtime monitoring for automotive electronic development. In: Falcone, Y., Sánchez, C. (eds.) RV 2016. LNCS, vol. 10012, pp. 462–469. Springer, Cham (2016). https://doi.org/10.1007/978-3-319-46982-9_30

24. Sneed, H.M.: Bridging the concept to implementation gap in software system testing. In: International Conference on Quality Software (QSIC 2008), Los Alamitos, CA, USA, pp. 67–73. IEEE Computer Society, August 2008. https://doi.org/10.1109/QSIC.2008.48

25. Walter, B., Hammes, J., Piechotta, M., Rudolph, S.: A formalization method to process structured natural language to logic expressions to detect redundant specification and test statements. In: International Requirements Engineering Conference (RE 2017). IEEE Computer Society (2017). https://doi.org/10.1109/RE.2017.38
26. Zander-Nowicka, J., Schieferdecker, I., Marrero Perez, A.: Automotive validation functions for on-line test evaluation of hybrid real-time systems. In: Autotestcon, pp. 799–805. IEEE Computer Society (2006). https://doi.org/10.1109/AUTEST.2006.283767

A Quality Model and Checklists for Reviewing Automotive Test Case Specifications

Katharina Juhnke[✉], Denis Neumüller[✉], and Matthias Tichy[✉]

Institute of Software Engineering and Programming Languages, Ulm University,
Ulm, Germany
{katharina.juhnke,denis.neumueller,matthias.tichy}@uni-ulm.de

Abstract. Testing is the key activity in ensuring the quality of automotive systems. The corresponding test case specifications often contain test cases expressed in natural language. However, there is a lack of review approaches that are easy to apply for practitioners to ensure appropriate quality of those test case specifications. We therefore present an analytical quality assurance method based on a quality model and review checklists derived from it. Especially, we focus on quality criteria that are relevant for natural language test cases and in the context of the automotive domain. To ensure applicability in industrial practice, we stringently involve practitioners in the development of the quality model via expert workshops. The systematic derivation of quality characteristics results in a quality model for automotive test case specifications. Furthermore, we show how review checklists for a multidimensional review were derived from it. A first evaluation indicates that these review checklists support practitioners in conducting reviews and also foster the understanding of qualitative test case specifications.

Keywords: Automotive test case specifications · Quality model · Review checklists · Formal review · Goal question metric

1 Introduction

Test case specifications in the automotive domain contain the relevant test cases for a specific system or component in the vehicle. For system integration tests or system tests, which are partly executed in prototype vehicles by human testers, these logical test cases are mostly natural language based [8,14,16]. Juhnke et al. [15] investigated challenges regarding this type of test case specifications in detail in a mixed method study. They identified that quality assurance methods in particular were rated as insufficient by the practitioners interviewed and surveyed from the automotive industry. Especially, there is a lack of concrete guidelines, checklists and a general understanding of what constitutes a high-quality automotive test case specification.

To close this gap, this paper presents an analytical quality assurance method based on a quality model for automotive test case specifications, which serves

© Springer Nature Switzerland AG 2022
D. Mendez et al. (Eds.): SWQD 2022, LNBIP 439, pp. 84–104, 2022.
https://doi.org/10.1007/978-3-031-04115-0_6

as basis for the definition of checklists. It, thus, contributes to improving the quality of automotive test case specifications. To ensure that the developed quality model and the derived checklists are actually applicable in industrial practice, we focused on the continuous involvement of practitioners in the development process.

The main research question guiding our research in this regard is the following: *How can the quality of automotive test case specifications be assessed?* To answer this question, we divide it into three research questions.

First, in order to assess the quality of a test case specification, quality criteria are needed. Such criteria are typically grouped in a quality model. We address this in our first research question:

RQ 1: *What quality criteria must a quality model for automotive test case specifications contain?*

Based on the Goal Question Metric (GQM) [2] approach, we present a quality goal and specify five viewpoints that are relevant for the review of test case specifications. We use five knowledge sources (standards, general literature on test case quality, automotive specific documents, expert opinions from interviews, and workshops with practitioners) that address different aspects of the viewpoints to gather information for deriving questions and metrics to build the quality model for automotive test case specifications.

Second, this quality model should be applicable and useful for practitioners resulting in the following research question:

RQ 2: *How can the quality model for test case specifications be made applicable to reviews by industrial practitioners?*

We show how we use the different viewpoints of quality in a multidimensional review to tailor the review towards different roles in the testing process. For each of these dimensions, we define a set of questions derived from the quality model, which are summarized in review checklists.

Third, it is important to evaluate how applicable these review checklists are for practitioners, which results in our third research question:

RQ 3: *How do reviewers assess the review checklists in terms of supporting the review of test case specifications?*

We conduct an evaluation with practitioners in which they apply the checklists and subsequently discuss their suitability in an expert workshop. The results of this initial evaluation indicate that practitioners confirm that the quality model and the derived review checklists support the review of test case specifications while enhancing the understanding of a qualitative test case specification.

The remainder of this paper is structured as follows: In Sect. 2, we discuss related work regarding existing quality models for test case specifications. In Sect. 3, we describe our methodical approach to developing the quality model and its quality criteria. In Sect. 4, we explain how we integrated the quality model into the review process and finally, in Sect. 5, we show how our quality model and the checklists derived from it were assessed by practitioners. Section 6 summarizes the paper and identifies future work.

2   Related Work

Quality models [12], consisting of individual quality criteria, define how the quality of artifacts can be assessed. Up to now, there exist no explicit quality model for test case specifications in the automotive domain that takes into account automotive-specific aspects of test case documentation, compliance with functional safety requirements, or natural language test cases.

Zeiß [22] presents a quality model for test case specifications (i.e., test suits) without explicit reference to the automotive domain. The quality model is based on the ISO 9126 standard [10], which has been revised by the ISO 25010 standard [12]. While the product quality model of the ISO 9126 standard focuses on the quality evaluation of software or systems, Zeiß [22] argues that for test specifications the use of a specialized quality model is more convenient, since the vocabulary used differs and characteristics are interpreted differently. Hence, Zeiß adapted his quality model from the ISO 9126 standard to test specifications written in the Testing and Test Control Notation (TTCN-3), which is used as standardized language for the specification and execution of large test suites [6,7]. This includes the definition of metrics for a selection of subcharacteristics of the quality model, which are adapted to TTCN-3 based test specifications.

Athanasiou et al. [1] present a quality model for test code, i.e., test cases described by means of a test script language. This model focuses on three quality characteristics for assessing test code quality: *completeness*, *effectiveness*, and *maintainability*. The quality characteristic maintainability is subdivided into the further subcharacteristics *analyzability*, *changeability*, and *stability*. These quality characteristics result from the combination and mapping of eight metrics, which are applicable to automated test cases. The test code quality model from Athanasiou et al. [1] is similar to the quality model from Zeiß [22], as it contains a subset of quality characteristics. Moreover, it is also related to the revised ISO 9126 standard [10] and refers to test cases which are described by a test script language and do not contain natural language parts. This simplifies the application of various computable metrics, such as *code coverage*, which are not applicable to natural language test cases.

The quality models from related work [1,22] are both intended for automated executable test cases, i.e., executable TTCN-3 test cases or test code. Especially the quality model presented by Zeiß [22] was mainly developed with a special focus on the instantiation of TTCN-3 test cases for automated executable test cases. Accordingly, the corresponding metrics also refer to executable test code. However, our approach considers natural language based test case specifications in the automotive domain that do not necessarily have to be executable automatically. In addition, both quality models are based on the outdated ISO 9126 standard [10] and do not contain any automotive-specific quality characteristics, so that they are unsuitable for the application to automotive test case specifications. Hence, it seems appropriate to develop a new quality model for automotive test case specifications.

3 Developing a Quality Model for Automotive Test Case Specifications

We used the general structure of a quality model (cf. ISO 25010 [12]) and the systematic Goal Question Metric (GQM) approach according to Basili et al. [2] to develop a quality model for automotive test case specifications. In this section, we describe how we applied the GQM approach and the resulting quality model.

3.1 Application of the Goal Question Metric (GQM) Approach

Following the template of Basili et al. [2], we define the overall quality goal:

> *"Improve* (purpose) *quality aspects* (issue) *of automotive test case specifications* (object: product) *from a methodical view, test plan view, requirements view, test platform view, and functional safety view* (viewpoint)."

Our *object* of measurement is an automotive test case specification for a specific system that is to be classified as a *product*. The *purpose* and *issue* of a quality model is to improve the quality of such specifications. To achieve this, it is necessary to consider the quality from different perspectives, as there are different consumers that work with the test case specification, such as test designers, functional safety assessors, or testers (*viewpoints*). These different consumers have different demands for, respectively views on, a qualitative test case specification. We describe the five review views including exemplary requirements for a qualitative test case specification in Table 1.

Based on the defined review views (cf. Table 1) and the quality goal, we specified a set of questions and metrics to assess the quality. To do this, we used the following five different sources of knowledge (I–V), which in turn address different aspects of each review view (*viewpoint*).

Source I: ISO 29119 – The ISO 29119 standard [11] defines vocabulary, processes, documentation and techniques for software testing. Part 3 of the standard explicitly refers to test documentation, which includes the test case specification.

Source II: General Literature on Test Case Quality – We identified literature dealing with the quality of test cases, reflecting the current state of the art in this respect and thus influencing the derivation of quality criteria. These include:

1. Bowes et al. [3] define 15 *testing principles* and best practices, which lead to high quality testing.
2. Meszaros et al. [18] define 12 *test case qualities*.
3. Hauptmann et al. [8] define 7 *Natural Language Test Smells (NLTS)* based on their experience from the industrial environment.
4. Petunova et al. [19] define 14 *questions for the assessment of test cases* and present them in a checklist for test case reviews.

Table 1. Review views with exemplary view-specific quality requirements

Review view (*Role*)	Examples of quality requirements
Methodical View (*Methodologist*)	Compliance with company- or project-specific guidelines for the creation and documentation of test case specifications, e.g., compliance with templates
Test Plan View (*Test Manager*)	Focus is on the implementation of the test strategy defined in the test plan, e.g., the correct derivation of test cases according to the given test case derivation procedures, prioritization of test cases, or creation of test cases to achieve specific test goals
Requirements View (*Department*)	Focus is on ensuring that all functionalities in the requirements specification are covered by test cases and that test cases correspond to the content of the requirements
Test Platform View (*Tester*)	Focus is on the feasibility of test cases with respect to a particular test platform, e.g., whether test cases contain all test data required for the test platform or whether a test case can be executed resource-efficiently on the respective test platform
Functional Safety View (*Functional Safety Manager*)	In a functional safety assessment the correct implementation of functional safety requirements according to the ISO 26262 standard [11] is reviewed by a functional safety manager or engineer, e.g., correct implementation of test goals and test derivation procedures

Source III: Test Case Specification User Guide – The Test Case Specification User Guide (TUG) [5] is a company-internal document of Daimler that contains guidelines for test case documentation. In particular, the basic structure of a test case and its attributes as well as the structure of a test case specification are described. This source is important because it contains regulations of an automotive company that have to be reflected in an automotive-specific quality model.

Source IV: Challenges – Challenges concerning test case specifications were summarized by Juhnke et al. [15]. These identified challenges are important as a source because they reveal certain problems in test case specifications that are considered as quality deficiencies.

Source V: Workshops – We conducted two workshops with domain experts from Daimler. The first workshop focused on functional safety (W-FuSa) as an important aspect in the automotive domain. We conducted the workshop with functional safety experts from various departments during a regular meeting of the functional safety committee at Daimler. A total of nine functional safety experts participated, who work as functional safety managers, conduct functional safety assessments or are responsible for process and method guidelines concerning functional safety in the company. The guiding question of the workshop was: *"Which aspects have to be examined from a functional safety point of view in a test case specification review?"*. We discussed different aspects with the workshop participants, partly using examples confirmed or supplemented by the experts. The results of the workshop are summarized in Table 2. Particularly, due to the ISO 26262 standard [11], great importance is attached to the relationship between test plan and test case specification, which is reflected by the results W-FuSa01 to W-FuSa04 of the workshop. Furthermore, the test coverage of safety requirements (W-FuSa05), the documentation of the test case derivation procedure (W-FuSa06), the test type (W-FuSa07) as well as the priority (W-FuSa08 and WFuSa09) were emphasized by the functional safety experts.

Table 2. Results from the workshop with functional safety experts

ID	Quality Aspect mentioned by the Functional Safety Experts
(A) Aspects to be considered with regard to the test plan	
W-FuSa01	The test goal has to be defined for safety-relevant test cases according to the test goals specified in the test plan.
W-FuSa02	The test case derivation procedures specified in the test plan have been used for deriving test cases.
W-FuSa03	The test case specification has to fulfill the test coverage required in the test plan.
W-FuSa04	Test cases have to be specified for each function to be tested.
(B) Traceability between test cases and requirements	
W-FuSa05	For all testable safety requirements exist test cases.
(C) Test case attributes and meta data to be specified	
W-FuSa06	The test case derivation procedure has to be documented for safety-relevant test cases.
W-FuSa07	The test type has to be documented for safety-relevant test cases.
W-FuSa08	The priority has to be documented for safety relevant test cases.
W-FuSa09	The priority of safety-relevant test cases is set to the highest possible priority.

The second workshop focused on the demands of testers (W-Testers), since they are the main consumers of test case specifications. Therefore, we conducted a workshop with five testing experts, who review and implement test cases as well as document test results. Four of the workshop participants have already been working in their current position for four to five years and one for more than eleven years. In addition, four of the workshop participants have an ISTQB® Certification Tester Foundation Level. The quality of the test case specifications currently processed by the workshop participants was rated with 3.8 from a scale of 1 (very good) to 5 (very poor), confirming the predominant quality problem with test case specifications. The aim of the workshop was to discuss the questions: *"What is a qualitative test case from a tester's point of view?"* and *"What are typical findings for testers in a review?"*.

Table 3. Results from the workshop with testing experts

ID	Quality Aspect mentioned by the Testing Experts
W-Tester01	The defined preconditions of a test case have to be complete.
W-Tester02	The defined preconditions do not contain any unnecessary preconditions.
W-Tester03	The defined preconditions of a test case have to be consistent, i.e., configurations that have already been made are not overwritten by a subsequent precondition
W-Tester04	The sequence of the defined preconditions is logical and executable.
W-Tester05	The defined preconditions bring the test object into the state required for test execution.
W-Tester06	Test cases for the corresponding test platform must be included in the test case specification.
W-Tester07	The test cases have to be potentially executable with the test technologies typical for the respective test platform.
W-Tester08	Ideally, the test case specification provides specific information for the tester, eg., test sequence, test configuration, model series assignment.
W-Tester09	The test case descriptions contain information relevant to the execution of the test for the respective test platform, e.g., signal names for the execution of HiL tests.
W-Tester10	The test cases can be implemented for the respective test platform taking into account the available resources, such as time or personnel.
W-Tester11	A test case covers as few functions as possible, so that errors can be assigned immediately and the time required to repeat the test case is appropriate.

The workshop was based on a total of 20 problems in test cases (so called *test smells*) that were identified in previous reviews from three different test case specifications currently being processed by the testers. The test smells identified in the test case specifications included too many, superfluous or missing preconditions, contradictory preconditions, test cases that were not suitable for the corresponding test platform, inconsistent terms and notations, very large test cases, mixing of actions and expected results, missing test purpose description, incomplete, vague or inaccurate test case descriptions as well as missing signal names and time behavior. 80% of the discussed test smells have an effect on the work of the testers, such as incorrect configuration of the test object, unnecessary testing effort, incorrectly implemented test cases, failed test cases or the tester is forced to contact the test designer due to ambiguities. In all cases, from the tester's point of view, the test designer is the person responsible for fixing the test smells. The other 20% of the considered test smells rather have an impact on the test designer, for example a resulting additional effort in the test case documentation in case of a refactoring.

Overall, we gathered the results presented in Table 3 based on the statements made by the testing experts during the workshop.

Based on the five presented sources – (1) *ISO 29119*, (2) *General Literature on Test Case Quality*, (3) *Test Case Specification User Guide*, (4) *Challenges*, (5) *Functional Safety and Tester Workshops* – and the GQM approach, we derived a total of 7 questions and 78 metrics. The following seven main questions (Q1–Q7) determine the quality of a test case specification:

Q1 *Does the test case specification meet requirements for completeness, correctness and appropriateness while complying with methodical guidelines?*

Q2 *Does a test case specification use information from other documents so that changes to that information can affect the test case specification?*

Q3 *Is the test case specification or a test case understandable for certain users?*

Q4 *Is the test case specification suitable for handover to the resp. test platforms?*

Q5 *Does the test case specification and its test cases meet special functional safety requirements?*

Q6 *Is the test case specification/are the test cases contained maintainable?*

Q7 *Is the test case specification suitable for further processing in the existing tool chain without loss of information?*

The quality aspects presented in Tables 2 and 3 were considered in particular in the main questions Q1 and Q5. For a detailed presentation of the questions, their metrics, and their origins, we refer to Juhnke [13, Table 5.4 p.138ff]. We used this result of the GQM approach to define a quality model for automotive test case specifications, which we describe in the next section.

3.2   Automotive Test Case Specifications Quality Model

We developed a quality model consisting of seven quality characteristics: (1) *Suitability*, (2) *Compatibility*, (3) *Usability*, (4) *Reliability*, (5) *Safety*, (6) *Maintainability*, and (7) *Portability*. Each characteristic represents a specific question (Q1–Q7) that emerged using the GQM approach and represents it with a specific term. The structure and some terms of the quality model are inspired by the product quality model from the ISO 25010 standard [12]. In the following, the seven quality characteristics are explained in more detail. Additionally, we illustrate each quality characteristics with an example of a metric. Due to space restrictions, we refer the interested reader to Juhnke [13, Table 5.4 p.139ff] for a complete listing.

Suitability (Q1) is the degree to which a test case specification meets stated and implied needs. This quality characteristic comprises the subcharacteristics *Completeness*, *Correctness*, and *Appropriateness*. *Completeness* is the degree to which a test case specification or a test case covers all specified needs regarding completeness with respect to various artifacts. *Correctness* is the degree to which the content of a test case is correctly specified with the needed degree of precision. *Appropriateness* is the degree to which the test case specification or

Automotive Test Case Specification Quality						
Suitability (Q1)	Compatibility (Q2)	Usability (Q3)	Reliability (Q4)	Safety (Q5)	Maintainability (Q6)	Portability (Q7)
Completeness • Test Plan Coverage Completeness • Requirement Coverage Completeness • Test Case Completeness • Test Case Specification Completeness **Correctness** • Requirements Consistency • Test Case Correctness **Appropriateness**	Co-existence	Learnability Test Evaluability	Maturity Repeatability	Functional Safety Conformity for Test Case Attributes Functional Safety Conformity for Requirement Coverage	Modularity Reusability Analyzability Modifiability	Transferability Adaptability

Fig. 1. Automotive test case specification quality model

a test case facilitate the accomplishment of specified tasks and objectives. An example metric for assessing the *Completeness* of a test case specification is: *"The scope of the test case specification is documented including typical pitfalls of the system."*

Compatibility (Q2) is the degree to which a test case specification exchanges information with other systems and contains all the necessary information for this. This quality characteristic comprises the subcharacteristic *Co-existence*. *Co-existence* is the degree to which a test case specification is independent of resources shared with other documents. One aspect of *Co-existence* is to ensure that the test case specification is self-contained and no links to external documents are present.

Usability (Q3) is the degree to which a test case specification or a test case can be read, understood or learned by specified users. This quality characteristic comprises the subcharacteristics *Learnability* and *Test Evaluability*. *Learnability* is the degree to which a test case specification contains or provides repeating structures or test case descriptions that support specific users in understanding or writing test cases. *Test Evaluability* is the degree to which test results or test failures can be assigned to certain test steps. The following is an example for assessing the *Test Evaluability*: *"Test cases are divided into test steps and each action can be clearly assigned to an expected result."*

Reliability (Q4) is the degree to which a test case specification or a test case are suitable for further processing and for deriving reproducible results. This quality characteristic comprises the subcharacteristics *Maturity* and *Repeatability*. *Maturity* is the degree to which a test case specification meets the approval criteria for further processing. *Repeatability* is the degree to which the same test case implementations or manual test case procedures can be derived repeatedly from a test case description. For example, to achieve *Repeatability* test case descriptions should not contain alternative or optional steps, which can be indicated by the use of control flow words like *"or"*, *"if"*.

Safety (Q5) is the degree to which a test case specification or a test case meets special demands for functional safety. This quality characteristic comprises the subcharacteristics *Functional Safety Conformity for Test Case Attributes* and *Functional Safety Conformity for Requirement Coverage*. *Functional Safety Conformity for Test Case Attributes* is the degree to which functional safety aspects are considered for test case attributes. *Functional Safety Conformity for Requirement Coverage* is the degree to which functional safety aspects are considered requirements coverage. A concrete aspect of *Functional Safety Conformity* is, for example, that for each safety relevant test case the test case derivation procedure has to be specified according to the test plan.

Maintainability (Q6) is the degree of effectiveness and efficiency with which a test case specification or a test case can be modified by the responsible test designers. This quality characteristic comprises the subcharacteristics *Modularity*, *Reusability*, *Analyzability*, and *Modifiability*. *Modularity* is the degree to which a test case is composed of discrete elements such that a change to one test case has no impact on other test cases. *Reusability* is the degree to which a test case or part of a test case description can be reused in the same or another test case specification. *Analyzability* is the degree of effectiveness and efficiency with which it is possible to assess the impact on an intended change to one or more of test cases of a test case specification, or to identify parts to be modified. *Modifiability* is the degree to which a test case specification or test case can be effectively and efficiently modified without introducing defects or degrading existing test case specification quality. Some indicators for the *Reusability* of test specifications are the parametrization of test cases, as well as the reuse of conditions or sequences where possible.

Portability (Q7) is the degree of effectiveness and efficiency with which a test case specification can be transferred from one (software) system to another. This quality characteristic comprises the subcharacteristics *Transferability* and *Adaptability*. *Transferability* is the degree to which a test case specification is suitable for the transfer to other (software) systems. *Adaptability* is the degree to which a test case specification can effectively and efficiently be adapted for different test platforms, model series or variants. To obtain a indication for the *Transferability* of test case specifications, we recommend to assess their conformance to guidelines and templates.

The quality model as shown in Fig. 1 has been developed with the focus on natural language based test case specifications in the automotive domain based on the current state of the art and current challenges reported by practitioners. Regarding the automotive domain, the quality characteristic *Safety* is of particular importance, as it highlights aspects of functional safety that have been confirmed by functional safety experts. The special feature of the developed quality model is that it refers both to the entirety of the test cases contained in a test case specification and their properties as well as to document properties (e.g., structure of the test case specification, documentation of persons responsible and reference documents used) and thus enables an assessment of a test case specification as a whole.

Overall, the presented quality characteristics of a quality model for automotive test case specifications allows an answer to research question RQ 1:

RQ 1: *What quality criteria must a quality model for automotive test case specifications contain?*

Based on various sources – ISO 29119, General Literature on Test Case Quality, Test Case Specification User Guide, Challenges concerning Test Case Specifications, Functional Safety and Tester Workshops – the following seven quality characteristics were derived: (1) *Suitability*, (2) *Compatibility*, (3) *Usability*, (4) *Reliability*, (5) *Safety*, (6) *Maintainability*, and (7) *Portability*. These are described in more detail by a total of 17 subcharacteristics as shown in Fig. 1.

4   Review of Automotive Test Case Specifications

We adapt the review process from the IEEE 1028 standard [9] and Spillner et al. [21] for the review of test case specifications (cf. Fig. 2).

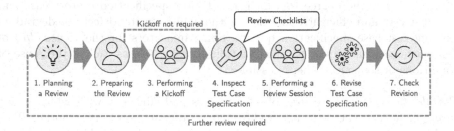

Fig. 2. Phases of the review process regarding a test case specification

A central aspect of a formal review is the Phase 4 in which the review object – the test case specification – is reviewed by one or more reviewers (also called inspectors). Checklists are a success factor for conducting reviews as they increase effectiveness [17,21]. Furthermore, Broekman et al. [4] see advantages of checklists in the field of testing embedded software, because the experiences of testers can be explicitly recorded in checklists and this knowledge can thus be used in future projects. Checklists are also suitable for formalizing information about an artifact to be tested and offer a systematic approach to conducting reviews. Therefore, the use of checklists for reviewing test case specifications is beneficial as they concentrate the reviewer's focus on typical problems and defects in test case specifications.

Our approach for the review checklists is based on the multidimensionality of quality [3,20] and combines it with the five different review views as defined in Table 1 at the beginning of Sect. 3. In this way, different review perspectives are taken into account for the assessment of test case specification quality according to the roles (e.g., developer, system owner, functional safety engineer, tester) relevant for automotive test case specifications.

A multidimensional review considers different dimensions, reference documents, and roles according to Pfaller et al. [20]. We define the following five dimensions in accordance to the review views: (1) *Methodical Review I*, (2) *Methodical Review II*, (3) *Content Review I*, (4) *Content Review II*, and (5) *Safety-Relevant Review*. These dimensions are primarily intended to assess test case specification quality in relation to conformity to one or more specific reference documents by a specific role. The focus of the dimensions differs as follows:

Methodical Review I (*Methodical View*) focuses primarily on formal criteria with regard to the applicable guidelines for test case documentation, i.e., the test case specification user guide [5]. *Methodical Review II* (*Test Plan View*) focuses on the fulfillment of requirements specified in the test plan that corresponds to the respective test case specification, i.e., the conformity of the test case specification with the test plan is checked. *Content Review I* (*Requirements View*) focuses on the conformity of the test cases with respect to the associated requirements. Both the correctness and the completeness of the test cases in relation to the requirements play a role. *Content Review II* (*Test Platform View*) emphasizes the perspective of the testers of the respective test platforms. It focuses in particular on the feasibility and suitability of the test cases for the respective test platform. *Safety-Relevant Review* (*Functional Safety View*) comprises questions on a test case specification that are relevant in the context of functional safety assessments.

Table 4 shows recommendations which reference documents are suitable for which dimension and which reference document must (●), can (○) or should not (–) be used accordingly. These reference documents can be supplemented by further project-specific documents and assigned to the respective dimension. For example, in addition to typical input artifacts for creating test case specifications, such as the requirements specification, test plan or standards, other documents that provide further information on the functional scope (e.g., network communication description, sequence diagrams, Simulink models) can also be relevant for *Content Review I* or testers of a test platform can also define their own specific demands for suitable test cases. Furthermore, internal guidelines, such as for Daimler the Test Case Specification User Guide (TUG) [5] or the methodical manual for electric and electronic software development and quality management (internally known as QMH), may be relevant.

Table 4. Dimensions for the review with assigned roles and documents

Reference Documents	Dimensions				
	Methodical Review I	Methodical Review II	Content Review I	Content Review II	Safety-relevant Review
TUG [5]	●	–	–	–	–
Requirement Specification	–	–	●	–	●
Test platform-specific Demands	–	○	–	●	–
Test Plan	●	–	–	–	○
ISO 26262 [11]	–	–	○	–	○[a]
QMH	–	–	○	–	●
...			...		
Project-specific Documents	○	○	○	○	○
Role	Methodologist	Test Manager	(Specialist) Department	Tester	Functional Safety Manager / Engineer

● recommended, ○ optional, and – not recommended reference document
a The comparison with the ISO 26262 [11] standard is marked here as optional, since the QMH represents the company-internal interpretation at Daimler.

Additionally, Table 4 shows that each dimension is assigned a role which is considered suitable to answer the specific questions of a dimension. Each role reflects a specific view of the test case specification in accordance with the dimension. An reviewer can assume on one or more roles. The roles *Methodologist* and *Test Manager* refer to reviewers who are familiar with methodological guidelines (e.g., test case specification user guide) and the corresponding test plan, so that a valid statement can be made about the degree of fulfillment of the test case specification in relation to these documents. The role *Specialist Department* refers to persons who are particularly able to evaluate the content of the corresponding test cases, i.e., whether requirements and associated test cases are consistent and whether the designed test cases are actually technically possible. This requires specialist knowledge of the System Under Test (SUT). The role *Tester* refers to persons who are assigned to an appropriate test platform and have test expertise in this regard. For example, testers can give an assessment as to whether the corresponding test cases are suitable for the respective test platform. The role *Functional Safety Manager/Engineer* is usually only considered for safety-relevant systems (i.e., systems with an ASIL classification from A to D). For non-safety-relevant systems, the dimension *Safety-relevant Review* can therefore be omitted and does not have to be considered for the review. A *Functional Safety Manager/Engineer* examines in particular whether specifications of ISO 26262 standard [11] were considered in the test case specification (e.g., application of the correct test case derivation procedures) or whether more company-specific specifications which are defined in the QMH have been complied with. Each dimension summarizes a set of questions specific to that dimension over the entirety of the test case specification. Therefore, each of the 78 metrics (for a complete listing see Juhnke [13]) was reformulated into a question and assigned to the respective dimension(s) according to the defined review perspectives. This means that each dimension and thus each reviewer receives its own checklist with questions on the test case specification.

In summary, based on the results of the GQM approach, a total of five review checklists were defined and provided as MS Excel templates. These review checklists provide reviewers with a tool with which they can systematically review test case specifications. The review guideline serves as a manual containing information on why and how to use these checklists. By providing the MS Excel templates containing the review checklists and the review guideline describing the concept of multidimensional review, reviewers are provided with a guide to assist them in performing test case specification reviews. This allows to formulate an answer to the research question RQ 2 in the following:

RQ 2: *How can the quality model for test case specifications be made applicable to reviews?*

The basis for the development of the presented automotive test case specification quality model are the questions and metrics defined using the GQM approach. These are used to derive perspective related checklist questions. By providing these questions in a MS Excel template, the different aspects of the quality model can be integrated into the review process. In this way, reviewers can use the respective checklist for the review of test case specifications depending on a specific review perspective (respectively dimension).

5   Evaluation

We initially presented the multidimensional review concept in two internal company working groups (with 14 and 11 participants) concerning test methodology at Daimler. It was positively perceived by the experts.

We additionally conducted a qualitative study to further investigate the applicability and usefulness of our checklist-based approach for automotive test case specifications and, thus, to answer research question RQ 3. In this study, automotive experts applied the checklists to real test case specifications for different systems. The study design and the results of the qualitative study conducted are presented in this section.

Study Design. The general task of the study participants was to assume the role of an reviewer by reviewing a test case specification. To ensure a high validity of the review, the participants were asked to review a self-defined scope of their own test case specifications by using the developed review checklists. Furthermore, this kept the effort for the study participants low and provided them with added value by participating in the study. The study design consists of three phases and is shown in Fig. 3. In the first phase, the participants had the opportunity to participate in a training on internal guidelines for test case documentation in order to refresh their knowledge on this topic. Subsequently, they received a preliminary questionnaire in the second phase, which was sent to them as an online questionnaire via the tool LimeSurvey [13, Chapter C.1]. After completing the preliminary questionnaire, the participants received instructions on how to conduct the reviews [13, Chapter C.2], the review guideline and the MS Excel template containing the review checklists. After reviewing the test case specification, participants received a final questionnaire [13, Chapter C.3]. Finally, in the third phase, the study participants took part in an expert workshop to discuss their impressions gained on the review checklists.

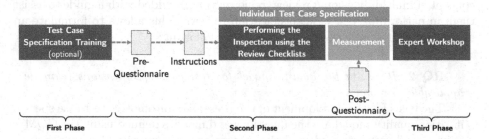

Fig. 3. Study setup for evaluating the developed review checklists

Data Collection. We recruited 11 test designers and testers from Daimler and external partners. We sent them online questionnaires, instructions and the review checklists and gave them 7 weeks to complete their reviews. A total of five participants completed the questionnaires and conducted a review of their test case specifications. Due to high expenses for the ongoing day-to-day business, the other six test designers and testers were unfortunately unable to conduct their reviews in the foreseeable future. As shown in Table 5, the participating practitioners were two test designers (P01 and P03) and one tester (P02) as well as two external engineering partners (P04 and P05).

Before conducting the review, study participants rated the subjectively perceived quality of the test case specifications they selected for the review on a scale from 1 (very good quality) to 5 (very poor quality) with an average of 3.4. The reason for this is that only one of the reviewed test case specifications had already been reviewed and approved, while the other test case specifications were either not yet finished, represented an intermediate result or had not yet been reviewed. Basically, the study participants would use checklists for future reviews. They stated that they wanted to do this sometimes (2 participants), often (1 participant) or always (2 participants).

Threats to Validity. Despite careful study design, threats to validity cannot be completely excluded, which is why they are considered in the following. To

Table 5. Overview of the review checklist study participants

ID	Company Affiliation (Years)	Time in Current Activity (Years)	Reviewing Expertise (Level[a])	Using Review Checklists	Responsibilities[b] C	D	I	R
			Internal Employees					
P01	11 – 25	< 1	1	no	✓	✓	✓	
P02	3 – 5	1 – 3	2	no			✓	
P03	6 – 10	< 1	1	no	✓	✓		✓
			External Engineering Partners					
P04	11 – 25	> 10	4	yes	✓		✓	✓
P05	3 – 5	4 – 9	4	yes	✓			✓

a Expertise Levels: (1) Beginner, (2) Advanced Beginner, (3) Competent Practitioner, (4) Experienced Practitioner, (5) Expert
b Responsibilities: (C) creating, (D) delegating, (I) implementing (R) reviewing test case spec.

increase *internal validity*, the participants were able to choose when, where and which test case specifications to review. This should reduce the influence of external factors on the causality of the results. In addition, the chosen test case specifications, working methods and work environment should lead to a representative sample of the participants daily work.

The biggest threat to the *external validity* is the low number of five participants since many of the other invited persons were too preoccupied by their day-to-day work. This can also be a bias in the selection. However, the study was conducted with real practitioners from the automotive industry who possessed a diverse range of experience, expertise and responsibilities with regards to test case specifications. Additionally, the multidimensional review concept was positively perceived by the 25 experts in the two internal working groups. Furthermore, the developed quality model could be influenced by company specific requirements. We tried to mitigate this issue by incorporating standards as well as other related work and keeping the developed process general enough to be applicable/adoptable by other companies in the automotive field. Regarding the *construct validity* the aim of our study is to evaluate the review checklists themselves and not any associated tooling. In order to exclude the influence of custom tooling on the feedback of the participants the review checklists were implemented in MS Excel since the practitioners were already familiar with this tool and using it in their daily work. To measure the applicability and usefulness of the review checklists the participants were questioned before and after performing the review. When the participants where inquired whether they needed further support in performing the study no ambiguities regarding the supplied instructions or the use of the review checklists surfaced. To strengthen the *conclusion validity*, our study results have been discussed and verified in a final expert workshop. This should mitigate the possibility of misinterpretation by the evaluators and ensure that the opinions of all experts are represented equally.

Nonetheless, we suggest conducting another study with a larger and more diverse set of participants to strengthen our results, e.g., in the form of an experiment comparing the quality of reviews with and without the review checklists.

Results. After applying the review checklists and carrying out the individual reviews of their test case specifications, the study participants answered the final questionnaire. The results of this questionnaire are summarized in Fig. 4.

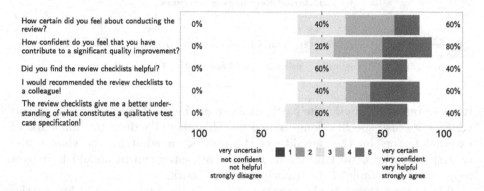

Fig. 4. Results of the review study

The results show that 3 out of 5 participants (60%) felt predominantly certain when conducting the checklist-based review. They believe that this has improved the quality of their test case specifications because 4 out of 5 participants (80%) are rather or very confident in this respect. Furthermore, 2 out of 5 participants (40%) found the checklists rather helpful or very helpful and 3 out of 5 participants (60%) tend to recommend them to their colleagues. Moreover, at least 2 out of 5 participants (40%) believe that the checklists contribute to a better understanding of what a qualitative test case specification is about.

In the subsequent expert workshop (cf. Phase 3 in Fig. 3), which lasted 1.5 hours, the impressions that the five study participants were able to gain from the review checklists were discussed. For this purpose, the participants were openly asked what they liked and what they disliked about the review checklists. Furthermore, it was discussed why the vast majority of participants found the checklists only partially helpful. Thus, positive and negative aspects regarding the review checklists were collected from the feedback of the experts.

Basically, the study participants got along well with the MS Excel templates, as they also use standard software, such as MS Excel or Word, for carrying out reviews. The following aspects were highlighted by the experts:

Positive Comments From the Experts on the Review Checklists:
"The checklists provide a guide that helps you not to forget anything."
"The checklists are good, because even an experienced reviewer sometimes forgets something."
"Checklists are absolutely helpful."
"The checklists encourage a uniform understanding of quality."
"The checklists give me an instrument with which I can objectively evaluate whether a test case specification is poor and show concrete things that can be improved."
"The checklists contain good questions, especially in the Safety-relevant Review."
"Helpful comments on the individual questions have been included in the checklists. The review guideline explains the concept and use of the checklists in a logical way."
"The checklists provide a structured guidance for the quality assurance of test case specifications and should be implemented as a uniform procedure within the company."
"The checklists should not only be used at the end of test case specification creation, but also at the beginning. The review of some initial example test cases can thus reduce additional work later on."

Negative Comments From the Experts on the Review Checklists:
"There are many questions in the checklist for the dimension Content Review I."
"The review checklist are too complex because to many questions are asked. This usually leads to frustrated reviewers and, as experience shows, to poorer review results."
"There are no specifications for tailoring."
"Many questions from Methodical Review I could be determined automatically."

Also, optimization potentials of the review checklists were discussed during the expert workshop. The main point of criticism was the complexity of the review checklists measured by the number of questions they contained. Especially if only one reviewer is entrusted with the review and has to consider all dimensions, she or he can quickly lose the overview. There is a danger that the reviewer will quickly become frustrated, resulting in poorer review results. The concept of a multidimensional review offers added value especially when different experts are actually involved in the conduct of the review and the checklist questions are thus distributed among different persons.

In this respect, the tailoring of the review checklists was discussed during the workshop in order to reduce the number of checklist questions. If several reviewers are involved in the review, the number of checklist questions per reviewer is already reduced because each reviewer only receives her or his dimension-specific checklist. Overall, the experts noted that the questions provided by the review checklists represent a comprehensive and valuable catalog which reflects current issues within test case specifications. In the special case that only one reviewer is assigned with the review of the entire test case specification and all dimensions are to be considered, this is challenging. In this case the reduction of checklist questions is appropriate. Accordingly, it was noted by the experts that not all aspects are relevant to each system or each test platform. Therefore, the checklist questions should be used as starting point and critically questioned during the planning of the review and adapted to the respective context.

A further approach to reduce the number of questions was seen by the experts in the automated answering of some checklist questions. Since in particular information on the questions from the dimension *Methodical Review I* can be calculated automatically, this is seen as a great potential to take the pressure off the reviewer.

The feedback from experts on the review checklists collected through the qualitative study allows us to answer research question **RQ 3** as follows:

> **RQ 3**: *How do reviewers assess the review checklists in terms of supporting the review of test case specifications?*
> The initial evaluation indicate that the review checklists have the potential to improve the quality of test case specifications by providing a comprehensive catalog of questions that indicate typical issues in test case specifications. In this way, they provide support to the reviewer in reviewing test case specifications and contribute to the understanding of which criteria constitute a qualitative test case specification. When planning a test case specification review, it is recommended that the scope of the checklist questions is checked and, if necessary, adapted to the needs of the current test case specification. Otherwise, reviewer assess the checklists as too extensive and complex. Furthermore, the lack of automatically answering certain checklist questions in the MS Excel templates was also mentioned as a negative aspect, especially for *Methodical Review I*.

The comments of the experts regarding the automated answering of certain checklist questions triggered the subsequent development of a tool called *QualiCheck* (see Juhnke [13]). *QualiCheck* can automatically calculate answers for simple checklist questions, which are then presented to the reviewer.

6   Conclusion and Future Work

Existing quality models for test case specifications are unsuitable for use in the automotive domain, as they do not consider automotive-specific quality characteristics like functional safety nor natural language for the specification of test cases. Following the GQM approach, we used multiple knowledge sources, including workshops with practitioners, to identify viewpoints, questions and metrics which are important to assess the quality of test case specifications. Based on our findings, we presented a quality model for automotive test case specifications consisting of seven key (quality) criteria. To facilitate the use of our quality model, we also describe its integration in a multidimensional review process derived from the IEEE 1028 standard and Spillner et al. We described the required process steps as well as the necessary documents (review checklists) for a systematic and thorough review of the test case specifications. The initial evaluation indicates that practitioners from the industry perceive the developed review checklists as helpful and would recommend them to their colleagues. Our results show that the application of our quality model is a good first step for improving the quality of test case specifications in the automotive domain. We discuss in more detail in Juhnke [13, Table 5.4 p.138ff] the extent to which our review approach is applicable to other OEMs. Future work should focus on the development of a condensed review checklist for the use in short reviews by a single reviewer and a suitable approach for tailoring. Additionally, the developed *QualiCheck* tool could be extended to automate further tasks of performing a review.

References

1. Athanasiou, D., Nugroho, A., Visser, J., Zaidman, A.: Test code quality and its relation to issue handling performance. IEEE Trans. Softw. Eng. **40**(11), 1100–1125 (2014). https://doi.org/10.1109/TSE.2014.2342227
2. Basili, V.R., Caldiera, G., Rombach, H.D.: Goal question metric paradigm. In: Marciniak, J.J. (ed.) Encyclopedia of Software Engineering, vol. 2, pp. 528–532. Wiley, New York (1994)
3. Bowes, D., Hall, T., Petric, J., Shippey, T., Turhan, B.: How good are my tests? In: Proceedings of the 8th Workshop on Emerging Trends in Software Metrics (WET-SoM 2017), pp. 9–14. IEEE (2017). https://doi.org/10.1109/WETSoM.2017.2
4. Broekman, B., Notenboom, E.: Testing Embedded Software. Addison-Wesley, London (2002)
5. Daimler AG: Test Case Specification Template 2.0 User Guide: Structure and Usage of TestSpec Template 2.0 (2018)
6. European Telecommunications Standards Institute (ETSI): The Testing and Test Control Notation Version 3 (TTCN-3) (2018). eTSI ES 201 873 V3.4.1
7. Grabowski, J., Hogrefe, D., Réthy, G., Schieferdecker, I., Wiles, A., Willcock, C.: An introduction to the testing and test control notation (TTCN-3). Comput. Netw. **42**(3), 375–403 (2003). https://doi.org/10.1016/S1389-1286(03)00249-4
8. Hauptmann, B., Heinemann, L., Vaas, R., Braun, P.: Hunting for smells in natural language tests. In: Proceedings of the 35th International Conference on Software Engineering (ICSE 2013), pp. 1217–1220. IEEE (2013). https://doi.org/10.1109/ICSE.2013.6606682
9. IEEE Computer Society: Standard for Software Reviews and Audits. IEEE 1028:2008 (2008). https://standards.ieee.org/standard/1028-2008.html
10. International Organization for Standardization (ISO): Software Engineering - Product Quality - Part 1: Quality Model. ISO/IEC 9126–1:2001 (2001). https://www.iso.org/standard/22749.html. (status: Withdrawn)
11. International Organization for Standardization (ISO): Road Vehicles - Functional Safety - Part 4: Product Development at the System Level. ISO 26262–4:2011 (2011). https://www.iso.org/standard/51359.html
12. International Organization for Standardization (ISO): Systems and Software Engineering - Systems and Software Quality Requirements and Evaluation (SQuaRE) - System and Software Quality Models. ISO/IEC 25010:2011 (2011). https://www.iso.org/standard/35733.html
13. Juhnke, K.: Improving the Quality of Automotive Test Case Specifications. Ph.D. thesis, Ulm University (2021). https://doi.org/10.18725/OPARU-35558

14. Juhnke, K., Tichy, M., Houdek, F.: Challenges concerning test case specifications in automotive software testing. In: Proceedings of the 44th Euromicro Conference on Software Engineering and Advanced Applications (SEAA 2018), pp. 33–40 (2018). https://doi.org/10.1109/SEAA.2018.00015

15. Juhnke, K., Tichy, M., Houdek, F.: Challenges concerning test case specifications in automotive software testing: assessment of frequency and criticality. Softw. Qual. J. **29**(1), 39–100 (2020). https://doi.org/10.1007/s11219-020-09523-0

16. Lachmann, R., Schaefer, I.: Towards efficient and effective testing in automotive software development. In: Plödereder, E., Grunske, L., Schneider, E., Ull, D. (eds.) Informatik 2014, pp. 2181–2192. Gesellschaft für Informatik e.V. (2014). https://dl.gi.de/handle/20.500.12116/2847

17. Lanubile, F., Mallardo, T.: Inspecting automated test code: a preliminary study. In: Concas, G., Damiani, E., Scotto, M., Succi, G. (eds.) XP 2007. LNCS, vol. 4536, pp. 115–122. Springer, Heidelberg (2007). https://doi.org/10.1007/978-3-540-73101-6_16

18. Meszaros, G., Smith, S.M., Andrea, J.: The test automation manifesto. In: Maurer, F., Wells, D. (eds.) XP/Agile Universe 2003. LNCS, vol. 2753, pp. 73–81. Springer, Heidelberg (2003). https://doi.org/10.1007/978-3-540-45122-8_9

19. Petunova, O., Bērziša, S.: Test case review processes in software testing. Inf. Technol. Manag. Sci. **20**(1), 48–53 (2017). https://doi.org/10.1515/itms-2017-0008

20. Pfaller, C., Wagner, S., Gericke, J., Wiemann, M.: Multi-dimensional measures for test case quality. In: Proceedings of the 1st International Conference on Software Testing, Verification, and Validation (ICST 2008), pp. 364–368. IEEE (2008). https://doi.org/10.1109/ICSTW.2008.28

21. Spillner, A., Linz, T., Schaefer, H.: Software Testing Foundations: A Study Guide for the Certified Tester Exam, 4th edn. Rocky Nook, Santa Barbara (2014)

22. Zeiß, B.: Quality Assurance of Test Specifications for Reactive Systems. Dissertation, Georg-August-Universität zu Göttingen (2010)

Author Index

Printed in the United States
by Baker & Taylor Publisher Services